For Daphne, with every
good wish from the Author

Alan / June 1997

MADRAS AND BEYOND

Alan Bourne

MADRAS
& BEYOND

Alan Bayne

The Book Guild Ltd.
Sussex, England

The Book Guild Ltd.
25 High Street,
Lewes, Sussex

First published 1993
© Alan Bayne 1993
Set in Baskerville
Typesetting by QBF Typesetting,
Salisbury, Wiltshire
Printed in Great Britain by
Antony Rowe Ltd.
Chippenham. Wiltshire.

A catalogue record for this book is
available from the British Library

ISBN 0 86332 862 8

CONTENTS

List of Centre Section Photographs

Vivian Collins in 1910 before the Teram Kangri expedition
The start of the Bombay to Poona trials in 1908
The author's father in Pondicherry, South India, 1906
East Coast Jungle, in Ceylon, 1935
The author's mother in her twenties
The author's father, in Bombay
Colombo-Madras crews, 1937
The Cox, 'Comrade' Sutherland
The MG18/80 in Colombo, 1937
South West Monsoon Regatta, 1938
The author driving the Riley Imp, 1938
A home-made special in the Mahagastotte Hill Climb
The author driving an MG in the Bogala Hill Climb, 1940
Racing at Ratmalana Aerodrome in 1948
A reprimand from a Marshal
The author's servants at *Shalimar*, 1950
Mike Henderson in the Lea-Francis, 1950
His Royal Highness the Duke of Edinburgh, 1954
With the $2\frac{1}{2}$ litre Riley in Colombo, 1954
The Colombo Rowing Club Regatta, 1955
Moose when engaged to the author in 1958
The family at Fairclose, 1968

PREFACE

This book is for you, my family, namely:-

Ann, my wife, to whom I'm devoted and who, most unfairly and quite illogically, is known as 'Moose'.

Julian, my splendid first-born.

Andrew, for whom the word 'irrepressible' was I'm sure, specially coined.

Sarah, my darling daughter.

From time to time you have all been 'at me' to put down on paper some of the anecdotes I've recalled from my early days in India and Ceylon. This I've now done and I hope you enjoy the reading as much as I've enjoyed the writing.

A. B.
Fittleworth 1992

ACKNOWLEDGEMENTS

I acknowledge my debt to Judy Webb, my long-suffering secretary who, with great cheerfulness and courage, has helped me so much with this book. For almost a year her professionalism and enthusiasm have been an inspiration to me and, bravely, she has put up with me and my foibles with scarcely a whimper.

A. B.

AUTHOR'S NOTE

I have tried hard to keep the events recounted in this book in their chronological order but not always successfully. I have given way, too often perhaps, to the temptation of digression but I hope this licence will not detract from your entertainment and interest.

A. B.

1

Some Background . . . pre 1912

I was born in Madras, in South India, in October 1912 where my parents were stationed at the time. The event took place in hospital, which was just as well because I weighed ten and a half pounds and as my mother was small – just over five feet with a size two shoe – she must have had a rough time of it. On 6 November 1912 I was christened in the Cathedral Church of Madras by the chaplain, who seemed not too sure of his facts because he entered my name as 'Allan' on my certificate of baptism, crossed this out and put in 'Alan' to which I have answered ever since.

So much for my beginning and now I think it best to tell you about my parents, their parents and others so that my background will be 'painted in' so to speak.

Ladies first, and so I turn to my mother and her side of the family. Her name was Constance Ruth Collins and she was born in Bombay in 1879 where her father was manager of a British bank. They were strict C of E and keen churchgoers and I mention the C of E bit particularly because my mother was one of thirteen children, six girls and four boys survived the rigours of the Indian climate and the pretty primitive conditions of Bombay. The others died in infancy. Of course, one 'went to the hills' in those days to escape the searing heat of the plains during the hot weather months. Most of the family were musical and after church on Sunday evenings young men used to be asked back to supper and music. This was how my mother met my father but more of that anon.

11

As far as I know, none of my maternal aunts worked ('not done, dear, in India!') One of my maternal uncles was in the Indian Civil Service, in the survey department, and one was chief accountant of the BB and CIR (Bombay, Baroda and Central Indian Railway). The ICS uncle – Vivian – made a name for himself in 1912 whilst he was engaged in establishing the heights of various peaks in the Himalayan ranges for the Survey Department of India. His most famous exploit is described in the *Alpine Journal* of August 1912 as follows:

Mr V D B Collins, Survey of India, has returned from Ladakh after making a series of trigonometrical determinations of the heights of Dr Longstaff's peak Teram Kangri. Mr Collins' triangulation was based on the Kashmere triangulation of Colonel Montgomerie and he had calculated the height of Teram Kangri from four different stations of observation. He makes the height of the peak about 24,300 feet. Mr Collins' highest ascent was to 21,000 feet but he did not take observations from this point. His highest station of observation was the peak of Shan Puk which is 20,288 feet high. At Shan Puk Mr Collins remained encamped for six days, his camp was pitched a little below the summit of Shan Puk and was at an altitude of about 20,000 feet. For six days and nights he had to remain here alone, unable to take observations, owing to the prevalence of a continuous snow storm, but he determined to stay until the weather cleared. In climbing peaks above 19,000 feet Mr Collins had to cut steps in the ice and as he had no previous experience of ice craft, and had never accompanied a professional mountaineer, his success can only be attributed to his own enterprise and pluck. Amongst members of the Survey of India now living Mr Collins holds the record for the greatest altitude climbed and his sojurn of six days and nights in a snow storm at 20,000 feet is an experience almost unique in the records of mountaineering.

Soon after the article appeared Dr Tom Longstaff, who claimed Teram Kangri as 'his peak', challenged my uncle's figures, whereupon Vivian Collins sent him his full calculations. On receipt of the figures, Tom Longstaff wrote from Brockenhurst in Hampshire:

> Dear Mr Collins, please allow me – as a mere mountaineer – to congratulate you most heartily over the work you've done on Teram Kangri. You must have had an infernal time waiting up there for the weather to clear. I really can't be expected to regret my mistake when it has led to such a fine bit of extension of that most marvellous peak. I need hardly say I accept your conclusions as quite final.

Of course, 24,300 feet is not all that lower than Everest and I still have Vivian's ice-axe and other paraphernalia he took with him.

Later on Vivian was working in the Assam States, north-east of Bengal, and he became friendly with the maharajah there. After some months my uncle's work was finished and the maharajah sent for him. 'Collins Sahib,' he said, 'you will soon be leaving us to go back to India and I shall be very sorry to see you go. I would like you to take away a small present from me in recognition of your good work and as a reminder of our friendship.' My uncle was duly impressed and wondered what the present would be. Imagine his horror when a child of about twelve years old was produced – this was the maharajah's youngest daughter. With considerable presence of mind Vivian explained that he had a most jealous wife in England, a veritable horror who would make the little girl's life a misery. All lies of, course – he was a bachelor. He went on to explain how deeply grateful he was that the maharajah thought so highly of him and hoped he would not be offended by his apparent ingratitude in declining the gift. My uncle added that if the maharajah really wanted to give him a present, he would love to have the sword he was wearing. The old boy was delighted and we still have the sword with us at Sorrels House.

That is all I can recollect about Vivian – whom I never met – and he was killed in action near Neuve Chapelle 9 May 1915 serving with the 2nd/2nd Gurkhas (King Edward VII's Own).

My mother's family were quite well-connected and one of her ancestors was Sir Thomas Munro – Governor of Madras. He secured his advancement by first being involved, in 1799, in the assault and capture of Seringapatam in South India and then, in 1818, as a brigadier-general, he led a division of the army of the Deccan in the successful storming and capture of Badamy, one of the strongest hill forts in India. He was then promoted to major-general and later was made Governor of Madras. The East India Company presented Sir Thomas with a silver medal in recognition of his capture of Badamy where, I imagine, they at once established their roots and set about adding to their not already considerable interest in India.

My aunts, the Misses Collins, were, with the exception of my mother and her eldest sister Eva, a timid lot so far as marriage was concerned. The four of them remained single ladies and this quartet was responsible for bringing up my sister and myself for five years in London whilst our parents were abroad. I shall have more to say about these good ladies and their brothers later on.

Turning now to my father – Harold Collingwood Bayne – I can say at once he was quite a character. Harold was born to Charles and Sophie ('Old Sophe') Bayne in September 1881 in Highgate. He had two elder brothers, Charles and Arthur, and an elder sister Ethel. He also had an elder brother Gordon who was killed in the First World War. Harold was therefore the youngest in the family and was known on occasions as 'Benjy'.

Whilst busy name-dropping I may as well say here and now that it was through Sophie Bayne (nee Schofield) that Admiral Lord Collingwood comes into the picture. Evidence is pretty scarce, and parents and grandparents were naughty, in this respect, but I am pretty sure that he was my great-great-great grandfather through the marriage of one of his daughters. We have items of silver belonging to him and as soon as Sophie married my grandfather the Christian name 'Collingwood' was given to all the males including my sons and me. I need not go into Collingwood's history because it is well-known, but I will say, only half in earnest, that they've got the wrong man standing on that column in Trafalgar Square. I say this because, as everyone knows, Nelson was killed in '*Victory*' by a French sniper before the final Battle of Trafalgar was properly joined and, as he was dying, he sent for Collingwood (or, as he put it, 'that splendid fellow Coll') who brought his Squadron of the Red into the van and took on the French and the Spaniards to their extreme discomforture, as is well-known. To digress for a moment – we had a French girl, on exchange with Sarah, staying with us a few years ago. One day I was taking her round the Trafalgar prints in our dining-room which depict the battle in some detail. Marie Annick – her name – suddenly went very quiet and I asked her what was wrong. 'Mr Bayne,' she said, 'I am thinking that it will be hard for me to go back to France to tell my friends I have been living at the home of a descendant of the man who defeated us so badly at Trafalgar.'

I remember nothing about my grandfather, Charles Bayne, although I know we met because there's a faded snap of him and my parents and me in the garden in Pembroke Avenue, Hove. I must have been one and a half or two years old at the time.

My grandmother – old Sophe – I remember vividly because she was still alive in 1920 when I came back to England from India for schooling. Sophie Bayne was a large lady and she always gave me the impression she was upholstered – well-upholstered at that – as she was invariable clad in black bombazine with a lace upright collar at the neck. She wore pince-nez and she peered at one through these with penetrating blue eyes. I used to be taken, or sent, to Hove to stay with Sophie for a few days every summer and I loved these visits, mainly I think, because of the quantity of food I was given. My four maternal, and maiden, aunts in London, where I lived, had no idea how much a small boy could eat but in Hove there were no such misunderstandings. One meal in particular I will always remember, although a lot of people find difficulty in believing me when I tell them about it. There were three courses and they were all pies! We started with a fish pie, went on to a steak and kidney pie and finished off with a fruit pie – rhubarb or apple or something. Never have I been so happy! Another fond memory I have of 30 Pembroke Avenue was morning prayers. These were said in the dining-room before breakfast and we all knelt at our dining-room table chairs which were turned round. The exception was old Sophe who knelt at a large leather chair and I used to stare at her bottom quite fascinated. This vast part of her anatomy – covered in black bombazine – was an awesome sight and she always needed help to get to her feet afterwards.

My visits always ended in the same way – my grandmother would call me to her side where she was seated and then start pulling up various skirts she was wearing. Finally she would arrive at a small chamois leather purse on a ribbon which nestled near her leg and from this she would produce a warm half-crown – always warm – and hand it over with a kiss. Half-a-crown in those days for a small boy was a lot of money and I felt very rich for days!

My eldest Bayne uncle – Charles – was a large man and I inherited a wonderful Holland and Holland shotgun from him soon after he died and I'll tell you the circumstances of this later on.

Charles's younger brother Arthur was a confirmed bachelor and one who positively enjoyed indifferent health. He had a rare peculiarity – two rows of teeth in the upper jaw and two in the lower. One would think with this splendid dental equipment he would get through his food in double quick time – not a bit of it. I would watch – fascinated – whilst a forkful of steamed fish (for instance) would be masticated, pulverised and ground to a pulp before being swallowed. 'Don't stare, dear,' someone usually whispered.

As I say, Arthur enjoyed ill-health and although he liked to be thought of as frail he was always ready to knock back a drink or two with my father and others. Arthur lived in Hove with his mother, old Sophe, and worked in the City of London with, I'm pretty sure, the National Discount Company. I remember being taken to lunch with him on one occasion and

16

then he brought me back to Hove by train. On the way down he told me he had done the journey so many times over the years that, with his eyes shut, he could say exactly where he was during any part of the journey. I thought this was highly unlikely but I remembered his remark many many years later when I was commuting to London and I then realised it could be done. The National Discount Company retired Arthur fairly early in life because of a suspected heart condition, and they gave him an armchair as a retirement present. He must have been an old fraud because I'll tell you later on how I came to his assistance some thirty years later when he really was ill!

At 30 Pembroke Avenue they had a large cook whose name I forget and a skinny maid called Mary. Mary was still there when I visited Arthur thirty years on and I have the fondest memories of both ladies on account of the way they used to spoil me at mealtimes! The final member of the household was a rather sinister cat known as 'Old Headache', which name suited him down to the ground.

My father had a sister, Ethel, a tall and most amiable lady who chose not to live at 30 Pembroke Avenue but had a flat not far away which she shared with a quite plain person called Lottie Thane. I remember Miss Thane had a dove in a cage which was called by a man's name until, one morning, it laid an egg so it was instantly re-christened Hilda or something.

As you all know I had a sister called Phyllys Ruth who was born in Mussoorie in Northern India near the foothills of the Himalayas. She survived an elder sister – Dorothy – who died in infancy. I'll be coming back to my sister, more than once I expect, as this tale unravels and for now I'll just say our personalities seemed to clash and we were at our warmest with each other when about 12,000 miles apart. Her affection for me seemed to diminish when she was about eleven and I about nine. It was Christmas morning and I had been given a pair of boxing gloves. 'What are those?' my sister asked so I dotted her on the nose to demonstrate. As I say, things were never quite the same again.

It is not easy to give a thumb-nail sketch of my mother and, instead, I'll set down various incidents concerning her as and when I come to them.

My father, on the other hand, was a spirited young man who was often in hot water (I have a son very like him!). He went to Highgate School in North London – one of the few schools, I imagine, who would have him. He was invariably in trouble although one incident stands to his credit. On holiday he was walking along a Hampstead road when he saw a crowd of men on the pavement who were having a scuffle, or so it seemed. Harold, aged about twelve, went up to investigate and he saw, to his horror, a policeman on the ground with a number of men beating him up. The story goes that my father squeezed through the legs of the mob, got hold of the policeman's whistle and blew on it with all his might. Help arrived and the poor man was rescued. Young Harold was commended for his bravery at a small police ceremony and presented with a walking stick of malacca cane with a silver knob. Sadly the inscription has been polished out over the years but we still have it.

Harold Bayne was boisterous and rebelled at any suggestion of discipline and things got so bad that he was shipped off, when twenty-one, to his elder brother Charles, in Kenya, who, as Harold knew, was something of a fierce martinet. This was not a good idea, or at least Harold didn't think it was, and after only a few months he decided he had had enough. So, leaving a brief note for his brother, he left the house one night, through his bedroom window, and made his way somehow or other to the port of Mombasa on Africa's East Coast. Once there, and being broke, he stowed away on a ship called the *Bezwada* and successfully managed to hide himself away.

On the first day at sea Harold came out of hiding and was taken to the captain whose name, would you believe, was Archdeacon! This was in February 1902 and Captain Archdeacon was not amused. He explained succinctly to the twenty-one year old stowaway that the *Bezwada* was not a luxury liner and that there was no first-class stateroom reserved for him. On the contrary, the old mariner made it clear that young Harold would work hard during the ten-day passage to Bombay, for which port they were bound, and depending on his work and behaviour he would, or would not, be handed over to the police when the ship docked. The message must have got through because my father's certificate of discharge, dated 13 February 1902, from which I quote, reads:

Conduct V G

Ability V G

and that was how the male side of our family first arrived in India.

Charles and Harold did not communicate with each other, I believe, for twenty-five or thirty years after the runaway episode and my father used to tell me that when they did meet for the first time so many years later, Charles' first words were, 'Where the devil do you think you've been?'

After settling down in Bombay, in pretty primitive conditions I imagine because he could not have had much money, Harold got a job in a bank. He then moved into a mess with other young European bank assistants. A 'mess', or 'chummery' as we used to call them in Ceylon, consisted of five or six young men renting a large house usually from a Parsee or other affluent Indian. Each young man had his own personal bearer and then a cook with his assistant were engaged to feed the whole mess. A gardener and dhobi were also employed and the young sahibs took it in turns, a month at a time usually, to order the meals and give the cook money to buy provisions from the market. In my day one's mess bill was about Rs 200 or Rs 300 or, say, £15 or £22 a month. Drinks were not included and each member bought his own and paid for his own personal servant and dhobi. In my father's day mess bills were, of course, much cheaper.

A large bearded Sikh barber used to visit my father's mess every morning at dawn and shave all the sahibs in bed. My father used to tell me that for the first week or so he would wake and lie petrified whilst this large bearded Sikh waved a cut-throat razor under his nose. After a while he got used to it and awoke every morning to find himself shaved.

There was a small beggar boy, my father told me, who used to sit outside my father's bank and call out, 'pice sahib – pice sahib' as the young bankers went to work. A 'pice' was an eighth of an anna of which there were sixteen to a rupee so it didn't amount to a lot! One day my father and his friends took this little beggar boy aside and told him that his 'pice sahib – pice sahib' business was no good at all and that he needed to sharpen up his act. They got him to say, 'Sahib – no father, no mother, no bicycle.' This worked wonders I believe and the little boy's cash flow problems ceased.

As in all Eastern countries, until quite recently, one joined one or other of the local volunteer forces – the equivalent of the British TA. My father joined the Bombay Light Horse where they had British sergeants and warrant officers to teach the young recruits how to ride. My father used to tell me how twenty or thirty young troopers would ride, bareback, seemingly endlessly round and round the tan (or drill hall) in a clockwise direction. When they were all dying of boredom the instructor would make a 'horsey' noise which meant nothing to the young recruits but a lot to the horses. These at once pirouetted and changed direction and started on an anti-clockwise circuit with disastrous results for the riders. The instructor would then shout, invariably, 'An' 'oo told you young gentlemen to dismount?'

The volunteer regiments throughout the East were invaluable, apart from being great fun, and provided an enormous number of officers, well-trained, for both World Wars.

To digress for a moment while on the subject of horses – about 1947 or 8 I was swimming one Sunday morning down the West Coast of Ceylon, at a place called Galle, some seventy miles south of Colombo, where there was a most glorious white sandy beach. We were all in bathing things lying in the shade when the resident ASP (Assistant Superintendent of Police) rode up, in uniform, on his handsome grey charger. Very smart they looked too. One young man in the party, a chartered accountant from Colombo and a good friend of mine, got to his feet and examined the grey minutely and told the ASP he had a very fine stallion. Well, this young man – one Tim Pontin –

was skin and bone and although over six feet tall weighed, I imagine, not more than ten stone. He was quite white and cut an unimpressive figure.

The ASP, John Manning by name, and a good friend too, was amused, I think, by this pale young stripling examining his charger and said, 'He's quite a handful but do have a ride if you care to.' Well, to our horror, Pontin said he'd love to and, still in his bathing trunks, got aboard. He dug in his heels and went flying down the beach at a full gallop for a mile before turning and trotting back. He dismounted, made much of the horse, and thanked the ASP. When he could speak the ASP said, 'Where on earth did you learn to ride like that?' We waited. 'I was a trooper in the Household Cavalry during the war, Pontin said quietly. We all collapsed!

My father (like his son and his grandchildren) was passionately fond of cars even in those very early days of the 'horseless carriage'. He told me once that he drove the first motor car from Bombay to Poona and I've seen a photograph of the event. The car was a White Steamer and the driver and passenger took turns to stoke the furnace and keep up a good head of steam. At the back of the car was a curious spike-shaped thing called a sprag and this was stuck behind or in front of a wheel to prevent the car rolling downhill in case the handbrake failed!

My father was fortunate in having the most beautiful bass voice (Uncle Arthur – with the teeth – had one too!) and he was deputy bass in the Bombay Cathedral choir. Accordingly, he was asked to the Sunday evening bun fights at the Collins' house and there he met my mother. I used to be terribly embarrassed years later, though still as a young man, sitting next to my father in church in Colombo when, as a mere member of the congregation, he used to belt out the descant of a hymn 'fortissimo plus' and people used to turn round and stare. I must admit, though, that it was beautifully done.

My father and mother were married in March 1908 in St. Thomas' Cathedral, Bombay and their ages are given as twenty-six apiece. I know my father's age, as given, is correct but alas, my mother knowingly fibbed because she was two years older than my father but was not going to admit to it. Whether my father was aware of this little deception on his marriage day I know not but he certainly found out later on.

My father must have done very well in Bombay because, after all, he was a penniless stowaway in 1902 and to find himself sufficiently solvent, in 1908, to get married says much for him. He is described as an 'agent' in his marriage certificate and he kept this description of his profession for many years. I know he imported things and sold them and so he was, in fact, a 'box-wallah'. A real box-wallah in India was a very humble trader on a bicycle with a large wooden box on the carrier. In the box were cotton and silk materials and all sorts of odds and ends which he would spread out on the verandah of one's house for the memsahib to see and, hopefully, buy.

Harold Bayne was a little grander than this, however. Although the nickname 'box-wallah' applied to most business-men in India, members of the ICS (Indian Civil Service), bankers and professional men such as doctors, lawyers and others were not box-wallahs. I say my father was 'a little grander' because one of my early recollections in Madras was his 'saloon'. His saloon was a full-length railway carriage divided up into our sleeping quarters, dining-room and draw-ing-room, etc. When my father wanted to travel, he would ask the Madras station master to have his saloon coupled to the Bombay Mail or whatever other train he needed for a particu-lar journey. I remember my sister and I were almost sick with excitement whenever one of these journeys was arranged. The train nearly always pulled out of the station in the late evening and so we used to kneel on our bunks in our pyjamas and watch the hordes on the platform milling around. We somehow felt very safe and secure.

Of course the saloon was only used for long journeys and my father used the ordinary train, tongas and bullock carts for his shorter trips. On one occasion he was touring by bullock cart in some remote part of India when he stopped for the night at a dhak-bungalow. A dhak-bungalow is a very very modest sort of hotel run by the government. They're pretty primitive and one bathed in a zinc tub and used a 'thunder box' when nature called. Somebody told me once that they were parked on a 'thunder box' unaware that there was a chicken roosting inside. The unfortunate fowl, not unreasonably, protested violently at the indignities heaped upon it and my friend nearly died of shock.

However, to return to my father and the dhak-bungalow – it was a very hot night and so he told his bearer to put up his camp-bed and mosquito net on the grass in front of the house. The dhak-bungalow keeper was not at all keen on this arrangement and warned my father that there were many leopards in the area and that he would be much safer inside. The good man was over-ruled, of course, and the camp-bed was erected outside on the grass. I remember quite well my father telling me that in the middle of the night he was woken up by a frightful growling and snarling under his bed. He didn't know what on earth to do and just lay there petrified wishing to goodness he had taken the dhak-bungalow keeper's advice. Suddenly the commotion reached a violent crescendo and two pi-dogs (village pariahs) emerged from under the bed fighting like mad. A much relieved parent was inside the dhak-bungalow in ten seconds flat.

We've now reached the time when I was born and so this seems a good moment to start a new chapter.

2

1912 – 1920
India – Early Days

As you know, I was born in 1912 and, soon after, my sister and I were taken to England to see my grandparents and other relatives. This must have been in 1913 or so and it was certainly before World War I started in 1914. We would have done the journey by sea, of course, and it would have taken the best part of a month. Ships in those days were much smaller and much slower than they are today and were coal-burners. Coaling in port was a messy business and I remember, in later voyages, lines of coolies, like ants, swarming up and down gangways with baskets of coal on their heads and emptying these into hatches in the side of the ship. We all had to keep our portholes closed.

My very first recollection of India was in a place called Nagpur in the State of Madhya Pradesh. I can clearly see to this day a very green lawn with three silver strips lying on it. On asking what these were I was told they were dead cobras with their bellies in the air, and then it was explained to me how they got there. Most of the big houses in India had wide verandahs surrounding the greater part of the building and on the outside of the verandahs we had things called 'chicks' which were screens made of very thin bamboo matting, or sometimes jute hessian, which kept the sun off the rooms in the house. The chicks were rolled up at night to let the cool air in. In spite of this it was usually very hot and so we had punkahs which were long wooden frames from which was suspended

24

some heavy material with a fringe. A rope from the punkah went out to the verandah and there squatted a punkah-wallah who pulled the punkah, in shifts, all night. He did this by sitting on the verandah floor with his back to the low outside wall and sometimes pulled the rope with his hands or, at other times, tied the rope to his big toe, crossed his legs and pulled the punkah like that. The contraption worked very well so long as the punkah-wallah kept awake.

To get back to the dead cobras – the punkah in my parents' bedroom stopped in the middle of the night and my father, in a rage, went out on to the verandah to rouse the punkah-wallah. To his horror, he saw the poor man, in the moonlight, mesmerized with terror, staring at a cobra coiled and ready to strike. My father had a long bamboo in his bedroom, for snakes, and he killed the cobra. Hard to believe I know, but it happened *twice* again that night and I shall never forget the story.

Something happened to me when I was a year old, or less, and although, naturally, I remember nothing of the incident the effects are with me to this day. My ayah either dropped me or let me crawl out of my pram whilst out on a walk. It happened in a village close to our house and I fell on my left eye. Instead of rushing me home the frightened woman took me into a bazaar shop and bathed the damaged eye to try and remove all traces of the accident so that my parents hopefully wouldn't notice. I can't recall any details of what happened but I know that the eye turned septic and I gradually lost all sight in it. The war then started and so my parents were unable to get me home to England until 1920. Once in London a Harley Street specialist – Mr Griffith – operated on me four times and finally delivered his verdict in 1922. He said to my aunts – my parents had returned to India – 'I will make it look like an eye again but he will never see with it.' I can't say it has really bothered me through life and, usually, I am embarrassed most when some unfortunate lady is standing on my left offering me the peas at dinner and the first I know of it is when my wife hisses, 'Darling!'

We lived in a large-ish house in a suburb to the south of

25

Madras called Chingleput and I have the happiest memories of our three or four year stay at Euandene – the name of the house. The ayah who dropped me had been sacked and in her place we had a dear old lady called Buddhi Ayah who used to spoil my sister and me something rotten – as they say these days. Buddhi Ayah never told tales and covered up for my sister and me whenever the occasion demanded. An Anglo-Indian lady of distant Portuguese extraction called Miss Diaz was our governess and I suppose she managed to hammer some sort of education into our thick heads. We didn't go to school I know and I'm sure Miss Diaz earned her pay and was glad of her holidays.

Next door to us was another European family who were very rude and very rough. They (the children) were known to us only as the mucky Babas and we were not allowed to play with them – something which we longed to do. I don't know what my parents had against the mucky Babas' parents but the 'no frat' rule was omnipotent. Who knows? – perhaps the M B parents thought the Baynes were so low – jat (badly bred) that we were out of bounds to *their* little darlings.

My father had a lovely car – or at least I thought so. It was an Arrol Johnson painted in bright banana yellow and covered with brass fittings which John the driver kept polished to a frazzle. A long brass snake, which was the horn, was my particular delight and it extended from opposite the steering wheel, outside the car, to along the front mudguard. A bulb horn, of course, and I adored squeezing it to summon the family before we went for our evening drive. The car had white drill covers over all the seats and these went to the dhobi every week and were replaced with clean ones.

We used to drive to 'The Marina' every evening when my father came home from the office and I bagged the front seat next to John and my parents and sister sat in the back. The Marina was the esplanade along the sea-front and there were always people there selling the most super things. Indian sweets ('No dear – you'll only get ill'), marvellous paper kites ('No dear – they break very easily'), super model ships made of papier-mâché ('No dear – they melt if you put them in water')

26

and all sorts of other 'No dears'. My sister's 'No dears' took the form of glass bangles, dolls and other goodies.

The oil installations were at some distance from the Marina and, one morning, I remember my parents told me that they had been awake all night because the German cruiser *Emden* had called and bombarded the oil tanks, setting them on fire before sailing away unscathed. I suppose this was about 1916 or so.

To digress again, (tell me if you get bored with these digressions) a much later *Emden* called at Galle harbour, Ceylon, in the early '50s. She was at anchor for ten days or so and the German sailors had a whale of a time ashore in the way that all sailors do when they're ashore. A great friend of mine called Jack Reeves – you'll hear a lot more about this scoundrel later on – told me that nine months after the *Emden* had sailed away the Galle hospital was crammed with little khaki-coloured babies with bright blue eyes! Oh well – sailors will be sailors!

Now back to Madras – I was about four or five and having my afternoon nap when apparently I awoke in a great state yelling, 'They're killing my Daddy! – they're killing my Daddy!' Well, this upset my mother a lot because my father was on tour at the time and there was no way in which she could communicate with him. Well, anyway, he came home safe and sound a few days later and whilst chatting that evening he remarked to my mother that he had had a narrow squeak. Apparently he had had his lunch by the side of a tank (a small lake) and when he had finished he put his back against a tree and lit his pipe. This caused some annoyance to a nest of hornets above his head (they say seven stings kill a man) and they swarmed down to show their displeasure. All my poor father could do was to rush down to the tank and jump in. Here he had to stay under water for ages I believe – popping his head up for mouthfuls of air at frequent intervals. Finally the hornets got bored and called off the attack and my father continued with his box-wallah activities. It transpired that the incident was at the exact time I had had my screaming fit. It seems I could have made a fortune as a clairvoyant!

Our servants mostly spoke Hindustani and my sister and I were fluent and so were our parents. Some of the servants, however, like the sweepers and malis (gardeners) were from the southern most part of India and spoke Tamil. My sister and I were under the strictest orders that on no account would we speak Tamil. The reason given was that it would affect our accent and make us sound 'chee-chee'. This was potty because, in speaking Hindustani, our English must have been as 'chee-chee' as hell anyway. This, in fact, was the case because when I went to my prep school in London my friends stared at me in amazement and wondered what on earth language I was speaking!

Our senior servants like my father's bearer wore white coats up to their chins with brass buttons and white trousers over bare feet. They wore wide cummerbunds round their middles and on their heads they wore white turbans with a diagonal sash of the same colour as the cummerbund. Very smart they were too. They addressed my father as 'Sahib', my mother as 'Memsahib', my sister as 'Missy Sahib' and me as 'Chota Sahib'. In Hindustani 'chota' is little or small and 'burra' is big. I never heard my father order a 'chota' whisky. The servants mostly spoke to us in Hindustani but when they had a grievance they went to a petition writer in the village and he wrote a letter for them in English. Quaint English it was too. My father once sacked a gardener and this worthy was most upset and galloped off to the petition writer to set out his case for him. The letter ended 'and I ask for these favours in the name of J Christ Esquire to whom your honour bears a striking resemblance.' He got his job back.

My mother's eldest sister, Eva, lived in Bangalore and she was married to a most charming man called Percy Anderson who was in the Indian Civil Service. He died in the terrible influenza epidemic which swept through India in 1918, killing, they say, a million people.

My mother, sister and I visited the Andersons once in Bangalore and all I remember about this was the ghost. This was a tall lady dressed from head to foot in white and she appeared, on occasions, in the drive at dusk. I never saw her,

28

thank goodness, but everyone else did including my sister (or so she said!). Ghosts were not my scene although, little did I know it at the time, I was to become involved with the supernatural for months on end when about ten or eleven. More of this later on.

It must have been early in 1920 when talk began about us all 'going home'. This meant England and the reason was to get my sister and me to London for our prep schooling, to get me to hospital for my eye operations and for my father to start his leave. The plan was for us to leave our Madras home 'Euandene', which was only a rented house anyway, and stay in a hotel in Madras until it was time to leave for Bombay from where the ship sailed. It just shows how primitive we were because my sister and I were excited beyond belief when we discovered the hotel bathroom had a proper long white bath in which we could nearly float! A far step from the zinc tubs we had in 'Euandene' and bliss for our ayah who, for once in her life, didn't have to waste hours persuading me to have a bath. I think it was at breakfast at this hotel that my father read out an advertisement from the paper he was looking at. This read:

Royal Bengal Tiger for sale – very fond of children!

The day finally arrived when we caught the train for Bombay and said our tearful farewells to Buddhi Ayah and the others on the platform. Then drama struck – we must have eaten some bad food on the train because by the time we reached Bombay my mother, sister and I were all violently ill and we were rushed to hospital, cholera being suspected. Fortunately it was only food poisoning and so we were able to catch our ship. This was the *City of Marseilles* of the Ellerman Line and I don't really remember a lot about the voyage. One thing I do remember (food again!) and that is that all the children on board sat at one long table in a sort of sub-dining saloon for their meals about an hour before the grown-ups were summoned for theirs. Well we discovered they had a sweet on the menu called 'rice fritters'. These were made of rice-flour and fried and were swamped in golden syrup and were quite

29

delicious. The boys at table used to vie with each other to see who could eat the most. The Goanese stewards were marvellous and entered into the spirit of things and brought us as many rice fritters as we could eat.

We arrived at Tilbury in late winter or very early spring and it was cold, grey and rainy and it must have been very disappointing for my sister and me who were by no means used to such dismal conditions in Madras. Within a few hours we were at 'Thornleigh' in Finchley, North London, the home of my four aunts to begin, I now know in retrospect, the most dreary ten years of my life.

Before leaving India, however, I must tell you the story of the Bengali babu and his boss in Calcutta. There was this Burra Sahib (a boss) in his office and he had this babu (a clerk) of whom he had grown very fond over the years. One day the Burra Sahib sent for the babu, whose name was Mukerjee and said, 'Mukerjee, we have known each other now for twenty years and I would like you and your wife to come home and meet my memsahib and have dinner with us. So will you please ask Mrs Mukerjee if you and she will come and have pot luck with us.' So Mukerjee says, 'Sahib, that is bahut atcha hai (very good) and I will talk to Mrs Mukerjee and tell you what she says tomorrow. But Sahib, what is this pot luck?' So the boss says, 'Well Mukerjee – pot luck is – we don't dress, we have nothing special to eat and, well Mukerjee – we want you to feel one of the family and see our way of life.'

So Mukerjee goes home that evening and confronts his wife and the following conversation takes place:

M 'Mrs Mukerjee, you know what?'

Mrs M 'No Mukerjee – what?

M 'Well, Burra Sahib has asked us to have pot luck.'

Mrs M 'Mukerjee, what is this pot luck?'

M 'Well, we don't wear any clothes, we get nothing to eat and, after that, they put us in the family way.'

To get the best effect persuade some passing Bengali to read this out to you!

3

1920 – 1924
Life with the Aunts – Oh dear!

As I have said we arrived one dismal, grey, wet winter's afternoon at the home of my four aunts in Finchley. The house was a three-storeyed affair and quite hideously Victorian. It must have been pretty big because it lodged the four ladies, my sister and myself, a cook and a maid and any stray uncles home on leave from India. There was, of course, my mother and father as well at the start.

Earlier on I called them my four maiden aunts – this was not quite correct because I now remember that one, Mabel, was a Mrs Lee. I never discovered who Mr Lee was but the marriage was a short-lived affair and to all intents and purposes Mabel was another 'maiden' aunt.

A thumbnail sketch of the four ladies:

Mabel: The eldest, small and very delicate, gentle and perhaps not the most beautiful lady in the world.

Ethel: Large-ish, nice looking and exceedingly grand in her outlook. Madly in love with the local choirmaster.

Enid: Stout, very affectionate and weepy and timid beyond belief. A very good pianist and her Cramer upright was the joy of her life. She was an A.R.C.M. I believe.

Merlyn: The best of the lot – the youngest with lots of courage and had a job with an insurance company in the City of London. She died on her ninety-fourth birthday in a nursing home whilst in our care. In her early nineties Merlyn developed an engaging habit. On her way upstairs to bed she would stop on the landing, look up at the ceiling and say, 'Lord, please take me tonight – but if you don't can we please have a decent day tomorrow.'

Soon after I arrived a prep school was found for me called Etchingham Park. It was run by a formidable man of God called, shall we say, the Reverend Snodgrass who had a sadistic love of beating small boys. Anyway, he beat me regularly enough and seemed to enjoy the activity. I entered the school at a distinct disadvantage – I should say three disadvantages. First, my parents had bought me the most sinister little suit in Bombay. This was a grey knicker-bocker affair with a Norfolk jacket – everyone else wore grey flannel suits with shorts. Then I had a wonky eye and, thirdly, I had the must excruciating 'chee-chee' accent. (My secretary, who is reading this manuscript to me has just remarked, 'It's a wonder you didn't turn out to be a delinquent!') My little comrades must have thought I had escaped from a zoo. Life at Etchingham Park was quite amusing and I loved the cricket, football, hockey and athletics. I was not so hot in class but then this part of my education was interrupted no less than four times for eye operations.

At one stage there was a sort of *Tom Brown's Schooldays* atmosphere which was prevalent. We had two bullies – one was half-French and called Verdier (he smelt to high heaven) and the other Bellman. Both used to thump us a lot and they had a whale of a time and succeeded in making our lives pretty miserable. But one day salvation arrived – this was in the form of a new boy called Egan who was enormous. Well, we little squirts rushed to Egan and poured out our troubles; I can't begin to tell you of our joy when good old Egan, without even waiting for another bullying attack, waded into Verdier and Bellman and settled their hash once and for all. I think the thing I enjoyed most at school was having other little boys of my own age to play with. In India our friends were few and far between.

32

I was a day-boy at Etchingham Park and I suppose this made sense because I was absent quite a lot having my eye operated on. A Harley Street surgeon called Mr Griffith did four operations in all and they were as successful as could be, except the eye didn't work. He had a super little sports car, an Amilcar I think it was, and it was painted in yellow and black vertical stripes so it looked like an angry wasp. I was in the Royal Eye Hospital, in the Elephant and Castle district of London – not far from the Oval cricket ground – and what a dreary dingy dump it was too. I was miserable and whenever my aunts came to visit me I burst into tears – they did too sometimes and so it was a merry little party in my room! They laughed once when I told them that the nurse had asked me that morning, 'Have your bellows opened today?' I didn't know what on earth she was talking about and they explained: 'Bowels dear, bowels – have you *been*?' Anyway, apparently the dreaded things hadn't opened because I was given the most filthy concoction in an enamel mug called liquorice powder. (The stuff was called that not the mug!) That did the trick.

I should have explained earlier that soon after we arrived in Finchley in the early spring of 1920, my father's leave came to an end and my mother and he returned to India for five years! A very very long time for a small boy to be parted from his parents. Of course, my sister and I were heart-broken and we felt so dreadfully lost and bewildered. Here we were in a vast dismal house with four strange females looking after us and we kept on trying the 'stiff upper lip' act with no great success. We were made to write a weekly letter to our parents in India and for the first few months we were only too anxious to do this. After some time though the exercise began to pall and this was I think because our memories of our parents became fainter and fainter and after three years or so I had no real idea to whom I was writing.

I imagine my parents paid my aunts an allowance for our upkeep. This could not have been over-generous because I was always hungry. Generally speaking I think maiden ladies have no idea of the quantity of food a small boy can eat and whenever I asked for more this was met with a polite 'No'. The aunts' logic was that they were bigger than I was, that they had had the same helpings, that they were no longer hungry so why on earth should I be? I gave up. Well not exactly – I would sneak into the kitchen and make up to the cook – a dear old soul whose name escapes me.

Going hungry was nothing compared to the exercise called 'paying the books'. This was sheer agony and consisted of two or three aunts dressing up like mad and setting forth to visit the butcher, the baker, the grocer and others in order to settle the monthly account. In my holidays I had to accompany them and my terror was that some of my school friends might see me. Imagine the scene – one snooty aunt, one fat one and one skinny one all dressed up to the nines and nodding and becking like crazy at their friends with one small boy (in that frightful little knicker-bocker suit) doing his best to hide from sight.

One day, following my aunts on one of these dreadful excursions, I remembered a discussion a small group of us had had at school. This was on the matter of how babies came. One boy said he knew exactly – he said a grown-up man and woman took all their clothes off, got into bed, did the most unspeakable things to each other and nine months later a baby came out of the lady. We laughed him to scorn of course and the mere thought of our mothers and fathers doing such things was out of the question. He was, in fact, dead right. But as I helped 'pay the books' and gazed at my aunts' bottoms the thought of them stripping off and having high jinks with a man in a bedroom seemed too preposterous for words.

Whilst on the subject of that dreadful little 'Bombay' suit, I am happy to say that the torture was not all that long borne. An uncle, one Trev, came home on leave, took one look at me and said, 'What on earth are you wearing?' My relief was such that I burst into tears whereupon the good man bundled me into his car and we went shopping! We came back with a proper grey flannel suit, nice shirts, shoes – the lot. Uncle Trev never had any idea quite how much his generosity and understanding meant to one (properly dressed) small boy.

There was another uncle – Ivan – they had strange names, my uncles – but then, being one of a family of thirteen, I

34

imagine their parents were hard-pressed to think of different ones. Anyway, Ivan was also home on leave – I am not sure from where or what he did – and he was terribly good with his hands. Once in my holidays he said, 'Let's make something – what do you suggest?' I said, 'A boat,' and off we went to the shops to look for a suitable piece of wood. We found a small gatepost in a timber-yard and we carried this home and he set to work watched intently by a small fascinated boy. He carved out the hull first, it must have been twenty-four inches long, and it had a high forecastle which dropped away to a low cockpit in the stern. It was the most beautiful racy shape and the first time we put it in the bath it floated on almost a dead-level keel. After some adjustments the boat floated level and then fitting out began. My holidays were nearly at an end by this time but we went to a dream of a shop called Bassett Lowkes in The Strand, I think, and bought solid brass propellers, stanchions, rails, rudders and everything else and, finally, an electric motor. The *Stella Maris* as he called it was not finally finished until his next leave but I saw her again some twenty or thirty years later, a little dusty, but still the wonderful boat at whose birth I was present. Good old Ivan – who was anything but 'terrible'.

About this time, I must have been ten or eleven, my aunts became mad about spiritualism and as it was mid-winter they had all the time they wanted in the evenings to indulge in this, to me, terrifying practice. They used a planchette – a small heart-shaped board mounted on two castors at the back and a pencil point at the front. They put their fingers on this, first having placed it on a board showing the letters of the alphabet. The curtains were drawn and the only illumination was the glow of the fire and one small table lamp. The other rooms were cold and dark ('We must all economize, dear') and so I had no other place in which to escape. I should say that before each of these ghoulish sessions began they invited their eldest sister Eva who, sensibly, lived some ten minutes' walk away. Eva was said to possess supernatural powers – she was the Bangalore Aunt who had a grey lady ghost in the drive, if you remember. Eva was the 'medium' and the sinister ritual revolved round her.

The planchette would move, pointing to various letters of the alphabet and somebody would write down the letters which eventually turned into a message from some dear departed. It always seemed an eternity before these awful seances ended and an excited discussion would ensue about who had 'come through' and what fun it all was. Fun perhaps for my aunts but it was simply playing ghosts to me and I was terrified. Especially as one or other of my aunts would usually say, as soon as the lights went on, 'Alan, dear, be an angel and get my embroidery scissors from my room.' This meant two or three flights upstairs almost in the dark and I hated these errands for embroidery scissors or any other thing they wanted. I went upstairs quickly but on the way down my feet touched about every fourth stair, with ghosts everywhere, in my imagination.

Aunt Ethel, who was besotted with the local choir-master if you remember, used to go to St Mary's Church in Finchley with her sister Enid. Mabel and Merlyn used to go to another church elsewhere. Well, Ethel, in order to see more of the choir-master, offered me up as a sacrifice and I was dragooned into the St Mary's choir. I found it all too much – two attendances on Sundays and one choir practice a week. We got paid, I admit, about 7/6d a quarter which wasn't a lot but augmented one's pocket money of 6d a week (5p today). Then there were weddings and funerals and we got paid extra for these. Funerals were good value at 2/6d a time but weddings at 1/6d were unpopular. I rose to be second boy on *decani* (which, as you know, is the south side of a choir, as opposed to *cantoris*, the north side!) and my pay went up as a result. I hated being a choirboy because it seemed, to me, to be such a waste of time – on a summer's evening, for instance, my friends would be off to play cricket or something and I would have to stooge off to church. *Dear* Aunt Ethel was not popular. Anyway, her goings on with Ivor Richards, the choir-master, came to naught which I suppose was very sad but even that didn't get me out of the dreaded choir. I began to understand why my father stowed away.

On a happier note, my first headmaster at Etchingham Park disappeared – called to his fathers perhaps – and he was replaced by a much nicer character. I can't remember the new man's name but I do remember one splendid thing he did for me. One day he summoned four of the least obnoxious boys in his care and told us that on the following day he was going to take us to the White City to see Lord Burghley run. It didn't mean a lot to us at the time – except that we were going to miss a day's schooling – but it turned out to be an epic occasion.

We piled into the head's car the next day and off we went. The main attraction was the 100 yards (or metres) event where Lord Burghley (later the Marquess of Exeter) was to hurdle against Harold Abrahams and, as you can imagine, those early thrills and memories of that famous contest were re-captured when I saw 'Chariots of Fire' so many years later.

My aunts used to tell my sister and me a story against themselves. It seems that three of them were going somewhere or other by tram when an exceedingly ugly man got in and sat opposite them. The aunts giggled (they were still quite young – in their thirties I suppose) and said to each other in Hindustani 'Bandar ka moo', which means 'monkey face'. They knew they were quite safe because it was a million to one chance that anyone else on the tram understood Hindustani. Picture their horror and embarrassment when the gentleman got up to leave, he bowed before them, raised his hat and said 'Bandar salaam karo!' (The monkey salutes you!) It just shows you can't be too careful.

When I was ten or eleven there was much talk as to where I would go for my public schooling. Many names were bandied about and I suppose the aunts were in touch with my parents on the subject. Enid, after profound thought, and with little logic, said. 'I think Eton because he would look so nice in one of those collars.'

However, there was to be no public school for your dear father because, in 1924, calamity struck.

4

1925 – 1930
Five Awful Years in Cheshire

My parents went back to India in 1920 after they had left my
sister and me at 'Thornleigh' with the aunts and after my
father's leave had expired. I am not absolutely sure what their
movements were once they returned to Madras but apparently
my father thought he could do more business in a larger city
and so they packed up and moved to Calcutta. Here my father
once again started up his agency business and he must have
been successful because the letters my sister and I received
every week were full of their goings-on. Firpos in Chowringhee
(I think), a cake and chocolate shop where a lot of the
memsahibs gathered in the mornings to gossip, was frequently
mentioned and I suppose my father was a member of the
Bengal Club and the Saturday Club (known locally as the
'Slap and Tickle'). My parents must have been members
because they were always talking about their club life.

About this time my mother had an affair with a young man
in the Chartered Bank, at least I think it was the Chartered
Bank. I know his name but I'm not going to mention it, to save
possible embarrassment, but I can say he was exceptionally tall
and as my mother was exceptionally short they must have
caused some amusement, as well as scandal, amongst the
Calcutta sahibs and memsahibs.

My father reacted to my mother's goings on in the most
strange way – he found the affair amusing! There is no doubt
that there *was* an affair because a few years later, in Cheshire, I

38

saw one or two bundles of letters tied up with ribbon and my mother got very coy whenever these were mentioned. As it was an old, and long since over, affair when I first heard about it I don't think I had any violent reactions, but now I cannot understand the calm way my father took it all.

So up to early 1924 all was well on the Calcutta front, except for my mother's dalliance with the young banker, and then *calamity* struck!

My father was told by somebody or other about a business, in Rangoon, that was up for grabs. A very glowing picture was painted (perhaps by the vendor himself!) and my father fell for the bait. They wound up their affairs in Calcutta and left for Burma and established themselves in Rangoon. To cut a long story short, two things happened simultaneously – my father got cerebral malaria and he went bankrupt. I can't imagine a more devastating combination of events to happen to any man.

There are three forms of malaria – benign, malignant and cerebral and their severity rises in the same order. I've had benign malaria and the name is a misnomer, if ever I've heard one, unless of course 104 degrees for four days is 'benign'. Cerebral malaria is a killer, literally, and my father was lucky, if you like, because he partially recovered after some days of violent fevers when he had to be tied down in his bed in hospital in Rangoon. Finally, he was discharged from hospital but the doctors insisted that, if he wanted to live, he must have at least seven years in a temperate climate. He had no choice – he was a broken man in two ways – physically and financially.

I've often wondered why my parents seemed so, 'unstable', if you like. They never appeared to settle – Bombay, Madras, Calcutta, Rangoon, there seemed no end to it. I suppose the answer is that as my father was his own master, and not employed by a company, he could do what he liked. They were both hedonists and liked to get as much out of life as possible with, I believe, little attention to costs or consequences. Profligacy must have been the cause of the fact that at the time he went bankrupt my father literally hadn't a bean. Well, only enough to buy passages home.

It sounds disloyal I know, but my mother encouraged my

father's extravagances and she was the most selfish person, as I discovered to my cost when my father died in 1945 just as the war was ending. More of this anon.

To return to my sister and me in 1925. Our parents returned from Rangoon and although my mother seemed quite fit, although naturally worried, my father was an old, old man although only forty-three at the time. I can't say I was shocked when I saw him because I didn't really remember what he looked like when he left us in Finchley in 1920. He had to look for work immediately because we had nothing to live on. Fortunately one of his earlier principals came to his rescue remembering, I suppose, all the good work he had done for them in India. Anyway, he was offered a job in Stockport, in Cheshire, and so off we all went. Once there my parents rented a small and very dreary little furnished house in the suburb of Bramhall and we settled down as best we could. All thoughts of a public school for me were abandoned, of course, and I sat my entrance examination for a Grammar School in Cheshire which couldn't have been very difficult because I got in. The school was first endowed in the eighteenth century by the Goldsmiths' and Silversmiths' Company and the buildings were very impressive with some of the nicest cloisters I've seen. Considering it was practically free, my education was as good as could be expected. In addition to the usual games, they played lacrosse at the school, which seemed strange to me, but I opted for the more orthodox ones and had my first introduction to 'fives' which I loved.

Holidays abroad were non-existent although I do remember a local one. A friend at school, called Albert Cole, and I had ramshackle bicycles and one summer holiday we thought we would like to ride to London and back, some 190 miles each way. My mother wrote to Aunt Eva in Finchley, the spiritualistic medium if you remember, and asked her whether she could bear to cope with us both for a week or so. Good old Eva – she answered at once and invited Cole and me for as long as we liked. We were nearly sick with excitement and poured over maps and decided we would stop for the night at Loughborough on the way down and Market Harborough on the way back. My parents made us promise we would not hang on to the back of buses going up hills. We promised solemnly and kept our promise. We did not hang on to a single bus. We hung on to lorries instead. We had a whale of a time as dear old Eva gave us some very useful spending money as well.

I left school aged seventeen and got a job as a junior clerk (office boy!) in a cotton spinning mill on the outskirts of Stockport. They paid me eighteen shillings a week (90p today) and I used to ride there and back every day on my bicycle. My lunch consisted of a 'tea-cake' and this was a North Country delicacy and was the biggest bun you've ever seen in your life. About three inches thick and five inches across, it was a filling meal – anyway it had to do because I couldn't afford anything else.

I had a great time at the Pear New Mill and my work consisted of, mainly, checking the invoices from the Egyptian shippers who sent us thousands of bales of cotton every month. On arrival at the mill the bales were dismantled and the cotton was weighed separately from the jute hessian and steel bands which covered them. The figures were given to me and I had to see that the weight of cotton was correct and that not too much jute hessian and too many steel bands were used to disguise a shortage of cotton. Some of the shippers were a bit dodgy. All new boys at the mill, as an initiation ceremony, had to walk round the perimeter of the roof. This was some ninety or a hundred feet from the ground and the perimeter ledge was, say twenty-four inches broad. It was a big five-storeyed mill and I suppose the total journey was three or four hundred yards. One had the vast drop on one side and a six foot plunge into water on the other. The water was for the mill sprinkler system and was in fact a gigantic swimming pool but filthy dirty. The initiation was not good for vertigo sufferers.

Of my eighteen shillings a week I gave my parents ten because they really needed it and so it is obvious they were always short of money and our lives were governed to a large extent by this embarrassment. Our delight can be imagined when in 1929 my father got a signal from an old friend in Ceylon offering him a job and he telegraphed acceptance right away. He sailed away first and in the summer of 1930 he sent for us.

5

My mother, sister and I were sent tickets for a BI ship called *The Merkara* and we were a very excited trio that embarked at Tilbury for our journey, once again, to the East.

As soon as we had turned the corner at Gibraltar the thrill of the tropical atmosphere of the Mediterranean was wonderful and I'm afraid no tears were shed at having to leave England. My ten rather dismal years were over at last. We stopped at Port Said and I excelled myself by buying a large bunch of green grapes off a bum-boat man alongside the ship. I hauled my purchase on board in a basket attached to a long rope, found a secluded corner and scoffed the lot. A great laxative, green grapes!

My mother took us ashore and we went straight to that marvellous shop Simon Artz. Here a topee was bought for me and I was very proud of it. Disillusionment came at Colombo when my father came on board to meet us. I was standing there resplendent in a tropical suit and my new topee waiting to greet my paternal relative. He took one look and hissed, 'Take that thing off your head at once and throw it overboard!' Overboard went my dear topee and a proper replacement was bought on the way home.

During the many years we lived in Ceylon (Sri Lanka now) neither my parents nor I ever bought a house. We always rented them and so did nearly everyone else. The only exceptions were the banks who provided rather splendid houses for

43

their senior employees and the diplomats too had their embassies of course.

Our first house was called 'Ardmore', in the Cinnamon Gardens district of Colombo, and it was huge and most beautifully furnished. It stood in the middle of a large garden and it was the rented property of an American dentist who was on leave in the USA. My father irreverently used to call it Pyorrhoea Palace.

Dear old 'Ardmore', it was such a complete change from Stockport and we lived there very happily for six months making friends and generally finding our way around. My sister, now twenty, got a job at once with the European nominated member of the House of Representatives and she was his personal assistant and secretary. I must admit she had grown up into the most attractive young lady and the young bachelors of Colombo (nearly 2,000) used to flock around; this to my father's rage because they nearly always called to take Phyl out just before dinner, stopped for a drink and took their time in departing. It happened two or three times a week and so there was usually a scene before dinner.

We had a number of servants, taken on from the American dentist, and my mother was in her seventh heaven not having to cook any more, or do housework, and generally reverting to something like her old life in India.

My father had an Essex car (an American gas-guzzler), a blue tourer and this held six people quite easily and I learnt to drive in it.

A man called Kitching, an acquaintance of my father's, ran a substantial hire-purchase company through which he advanced money to lorry and bus owners, and to private motorists as well, so that they could buy their vehicles on the 'never never'. Well, Kitching had had to re-possess a fleet of lorries because the hirer couldn't meet his hire-purchase instalments. Kitching suggested, that if I had nothing better to do, I might be interested in running the lorries. I was nineteen, I *had* nothing better to do, the pay was good (untold riches to me) and so I jumped at the offer. I discovered the lorries were chartered by firms in Colombo and elsewhere to take loads of tea, rubber, copra and things to the harbour and bring back imports from the docks. I was given a car, a square-nosed Morris Oxford of great age and my job was to see that all went well, that the drivers didn't sell things to and from the harbour (the 'fell off the back of a lorry' syndrome), that the lorries got help if they broke down and generally to try and make some money for old Kitching. I loved it and from a very early morning start until evening I was haring round Colombo and its environs keeping a fatherly eye on my little charges. Actually, I got very fond of some of the drivers even if they were rascals to a man.

It was about this time that I met Jack Reeves who became my greatest friend and who sadly died of cancer in about 1966 whilst still a comparatively young man. Jack was a few months younger than me and had just left Monkton Combe where he rowed in their first eight and he was a very good cox too. Jack was a good cox because he was slightly built; he was also a marvellous diver – the Ceylon champion for some years – and a good swimmer. A thorough wet-bob in fact, and any modest successes I may have had in rowing, diving and swimming are due entirely to Jack's patience and perseverance.

Jack was out of a job too when he first came out to Ceylon and so, on many occasions, he came out with me in the Morris Oxford whilst I chivvied up my lorry drivers. One of our better trips was when I had to go out to a place called Avisawella some thirty miles from Colombo. We had won a contract to bring rubber tree logs from various estates in the area to the railway sidings at Avisawella. You may not know it – there's no reason why you should – but after so many years – twenty-five or thirty I think – rubber trees become old, their latex flow begins to die away and they become unproductive. At this stage the estates (plantations) clear out divisions of the old rubber and plant new seedlings. First they cut the roots of the old trees and then the planters hire elephants from the villages who push over the trees with their foreheads. I've watched this performance for hours and I've never ceased to be astonished at an elephant's strength. The dear old 'elly' strolls up to a tree and with a seemingly gentle nudge pushes it over. They appear

45

to be so gentle. I digress (as usual).

The rubber tree logs, about twenty-five or thirty feet long and stripped of all branches, were then loaded into my lorries by the elephants under the guidance of their mahouts. They say that if an elephant drops a log and hurts himself he will not touch that log again and I believe this to be true. Once loaded, the lorries left the estates and proceeded to the railway sidings at Avisawella where a fresh gang of elephants would be waiting to take the logs off the lorries and stack them on the railway waggons. I tried hard to get the contract to bring the logs straight to Colombo by my lorries, thereby cutting out the railway, but I couldn't compete – the railway was much cheaper. You would like to know what they used the rubber logs for, wouldn't you? Well, so would I – but I can't for the life of me remember!

Whilst dealing with elephants and Avisawella, I was staying with a planter friend once on his rubber estate in the Kelani Valley district. Over that weekend there was a religious festival day – I think it was called Thai Pongal – and we went to the Taldua Club near Avisawella to have lunch and watch the celebrations. The main entertainment at the Club was a number of elephant races on the rugger ground. About eight or ten elephants took part in each race and it was the most spectacular affair. I think it was the noise that was the most impressive part – the noise coupled with the trembling of the ground as the elephants passed. Thirty or so tons of elephant doing fifteen or twenty miles an hour is an awe-inspiring sight when seen for the first time.

To return to Jack Reeves, again – his father was the vicar at Christ Church, Colombo, and Jack lived in the vicarage with his parents and his elder brother Cyril. Cyril was a fine athlete with an attractive singing voice, not unlike Nöel Coward. Jack's father was a missionary in China when he was born and, like me, he spent his early childhood years out East until it was time to come home for schooling. Whilst in China, young Reeves became an expert with chopsticks, as one can imagine. His favourite party piece when I knew him was to hold a pair of chopsticks in each hand, open a box of matches with them, take out a match, strike it and light his cigarette. We all tried of course but got simply nowhere.

My family all went to Christ Church on most Sunday evenings and my father became vicar's warden, carrying out his duties effectively when he wasn't deafening the whole congregation with his singing. My sister was married there and our two sons Julian and Andrew were christened there many years later.

By this time we had left the palatial Ardmore and moved to a smaller house a mile or two away. This was rented too but by now we had our own furniture and things. It was called Enfield and it was situated in a road called Ward Place. Now Ward Place almost connected the General Hospital with Kanatte Cemetery and practically every day a funeral procession went past our front gate. The dead in that climate had to be buried pretty smartly but the deceased's relatives always seemed to have plenty of time to organise a party. There were tom-toms, trumpets and usually fifty or sixty people on foot following the litter carried by the men. It was very very noisy and, at weekends when we were having our afternoon naps, it was very very annoying. We used to call Ward Place 'The Stiffs Parade', most unkind.

I suppose I spent about a year doing my lorry work when Mr Kitching suggested a change because he had had an offer for the fleet which he felt he should accept. He always made it a condition, when he financed someone's bus, lorry or car, that they should insure it through him so it follows that we had a sizeable insurance department. Mr Kitching transferred me to his insurance department and that is where I started my insurance career. My pay went up too!

Arthur Kitching, a nephew, also worked in the same firm but on the hire-purchase side. He was older than me and was the most wild and amusing character, and I admired him a lot. Arthur's job was to see that all the hirers (the people who had bought their vehicles on the never-never) were up to date in their instalments. If they were in arrears, steps would be taken to re-possess the vehicle and in order to be able to do this a staff of four 'seizers' was employed. I've said that Arthur Kitching

47

was wild – you should have seen the seizers, they were the most terrifying quartet I've ever seen and I was always glad I was on their side. One particular gentleman was almost sub-human – I mean, if he had been put into a cage full of gorillas he would have had to keep his hat on so one could tell the difference. I believe he was kindness itself to his wife and children! The seizers had to be tough, of course, because their job was a dangerous one and re-possessing say, a lorry, from an indebted (and infuriated) hirer was rather like trying to deprive a she-wolf of her cubs.

Young Kitching used to drink a bit – well, we all did – but he went a lot further, as far as attacks of DTs in fact. After one particularly bad bout he was sent to hospital to dry out and when he got back to the office I asked him how he was. 'It's unnatural,' he said, 'this remembering going to bed and waking up in the morning feeling well – quite unnatural.'

A last word about Arthur Kitching – he used to live in a chummery opposite the Police Training School in Havelock Road. The young police recruits used to lay their speed traps along this stretch of road and Arthur's chummery was right in the middle. Coming home from work in the evenings he would enter the speed trap at about fifty miles an hour and the little policemen would start their stop watches and jump up and down and wave to their comrades at the other end – and Arthur would turn into his front drive in the middle of the trap. Baffled constabulary!

About this time my father persuaded me to join a local volunteer unit – he was already a member. It was the Ceylon Supply and Transport Corps known affectionately as 'The Stout and Tonics'. I had reservations about joining because I felt that in the event of war I would much prefer to be a fighting soldier and not go stooging around in a lorry handing out bully beef and biscuits to the long-suffering soldiery. However, my cunning father pointed out that they had two armoured cars – Albions with Rolls Royce engines and that I'd probably be driving one of these. So I enrolled as a 'driver' and we had a lot of fun.

Every year we went to camp for a fortnight at a place called

Diyatalawa some four hours' drive from Colombo. We would go up in convoy with all our lorries *and* the two armoured cars and we would take it in turns to drive different vehicles. We also took our mess piano. There were some hundred or so of us (all Europeans) and once at Diyatalawa we were settled into long corrugated iron huts painted green and with stone floors. All the Ceylon garrison used to camp each year at Diyatalawa (The Royal Navy, when they called, camped there too – the sailors couldn't pronounce the name so they called it 'Ditty Wally'). Anyway we always had a great time, drilling and exercising hard all day and carousing pretty strenuously in the evenings unless a night exercise had been laid on. Diyatalawa was cool and dry and I suppose about 5,000 feet up in the hills and so the climate was wonderful for us poor Colombo wallahs.

Prince Henry, the Duke of Gloucester, came to Colombo once for a two day visit and my father and I, being respectively the oldest and youngest members of the corps, were given the job of driving him around. We were given a large Humber Super Snipe and my father always drove when the Duke was in the car and I acted as flunkey, opening and shutting doors. The one thing that stands out in my memory is that the Duke was always late for everything – but everything – and I think he enjoyed himself a lot. My father and I found it strange though that having dropped HRH at a party we consorted with the other drivers and servants till we were sent for to drive him home.

Every year we used to fire our course and this consisted of falling in outside the Maradana railway station early in the morning in full battle order – rifle, Lewis guns, packs and everything. Precisely, at a given moment, we would march off, section by section, to the firing range at a place called Hunupitiya seven miles away. Exactly two hours after we had started the targets would go up at the range, stay up for five minutes and then go down and we *had* to be there to start firing or else.

There were three main volunteer units in Ceylon in my day, all European, and they were The Ceylon Mounted Rifles, The Ceylon Planters Rifle Corps and ourselves. The CPRC was the one I hankered after (and later joined) and it consisted of two battalions – one embracing the planting fraternity up-country and the other the Colombo mercantile community. The CPRC was affiliated to The Rifle Brigade and we were very proud of our heritage. We wore the same black buttons, marched at the proper light infantry speed of 140 paces a minute and generally we were a real fighting force. I would say at least eight-five or ninety percent of the CPRC left Colombo in 1939 and 1940 to be commissioned into regiments of the Indian Army or finally any other regiment one wanted. However, more of this when we get to 1939.

As I mentioned earlier, Jack Reeves went to Monkton Combe school in Wiltshire and so did his great friend Phil Fowke. Fowke was a giant of a man, over six feet tall and he weighted sixteen stone or so and this was just as well as I shall explain in a minute. He was a tea-planter in a district called Ragalla roughly in the middle of the island and some 5,000 or 6,000 feet high. Like Jack and me he rowed and had a passion for cars. He had an Ulster Austin which was a very fast little two-seater sports car and with this he used to terrify the other road users in the district and himself too, at times, I imagine.

On the subject of roads – the up-country roads were winding and very narrow and, of course, very steep. They were tarred admittedly but the drop on one side was usually precipitous so one had to be careful, particularly at night coming home from the club, to keep to the anything but straight and narrow. Once one left the main road and entered upon one's own estate road conditions got even hairier – steeper, windier and sometimes not tarred.

Phil was immensely strong and once, when he was badly parked, I watched him pick his Austin 7 up by the tail and move the rear end to the side so that he could the more easily reverse out.

Whilst still a bachelor, Phil was woken up at 2 am one morning by his teamaker. A teamaker is the senior employee (usually a Tamil in the up-country tea districts) in a tea factory and is responsible for the whole manufacturing process of the tea from the time the green leaf enters the factory until the finally made black tea is sent away for shipment. The teamaker was in a great state and said one of the coolies had been found near the factory, bleeding badly and he believed he had been mauled by a leopard. There *were* leopards in the area. Phil thought it was far more likely that the coolie had had too much toddy to drink and had fallen off the very steep road into some pruned tea. I know for a fact that newly pruned tea bushes can be lethal.

Well, to put on a bit of a show, Phil got up, put on a pair of shorts and a sweater, got a torch and his shotgun and put two SG cartridges in his pocket. An SG cartridge is one which instead of holding masses of small shot contains three or four large lead beads and these will stop just about anything, leopard, bear, buffalo and even elephant if you hit it in the right place. He told the teamaker to lead on, which he did carrying his hurricane lantern. They got to the factory and there was the injured coolie lying inside and obviously pretty bad. On asking the other coolies looking on which way 'the leopard' went they all pointed up the hill. So Phil set off followed by the teamaker with his hurricane lantern. They tramped about through the tea for hours and as soon as it was first light Phil got fed up with the whole exercise – he didn't believe the leopard story anyway – gave the teamaker his gun, still loaded luckily (very dangerous habit!) and made tracks for home. He told me that he had taken no more than half a dozen steps when the leopard was on him. Phil was standing up and the leopard had its front paws round his neck and its teeth buried in his shoulder. Its back legs were trying to disembowel him. He went down fighting for his life with a form of terror, he told me, that one cannot describe. Suddenly there was a loud bang and he woke up in hospital.

Phil told me the whole story afterwards. Apparently, the teamaker was too terrified with shock to do anything at first and simply stood transfixed watching the awful fight going on. Then he came to his senses and knew he must kill the leopard without shooting his *dorai* (master). The problem was how to do this because leopard and planter were rolling over and over amongst the tea bushes. The leopard gave the teamaker the chance he was looking for when he finally managed to pin Phil to the ground lying on top of him. The teamaker shoved both barrels up against the leopard's backside and pulled both triggers – that did the trick.

Phil told me, as I've said, that the terror he felt fighting for his life against a wild animal far stronger than himself was beyond description. To give you some idea of a leopard's strength, Jim Corbett in his book *The Man-Eating Leopard of Rudraprayag*, describes how the leopard once killed a young and buxom girl weighing about 150 pounds and then carried her away from the scene of the kill holding her by the small of the back high off the ground. The ground was newly ploughed and soft and no part of the girl he was carrying in his jaws could be seen on the trail left by the leopard. Even when he jumped down a twelve foot bank on to damp mud he did not let any part of the dead girls' body make an imprint on the ground. The only signs were the four splayed pug marks of the man-eater.

Phil was in hospital for some time because his very serious wounds turned septic whilst they were healing and they all had to be opened up again and treated. The Ceylon papers were full of the story. I've seen the leopard skin and it was very big indeed.

If you remember, I said Phil was an oarsman and he used to row in the up-country crew which used to compete against a Colombo Rowing Club crew each year in Colombo. So Jack Reeves, Phil Fowke and I used to row and 'hill climb' (in cars) together and generally see each other pretty regularly. Just before the war Phil fell in love with a most attractive and charming girl called Joyce McKee who was a planter's daughter, in the same district, and I was very honoured when they asked me to be godfather to their son.

Whilst on the subject of wild animals – we had two fine game reserves in Ceylon – one was on the West Coast called Wilpattu and the other, called Yala, was at the southernmost tip of the island. I've visited both on several occasions – Wilpattu more than Yala – and have always been very sad when my three or four day stay came to an end.

I remember my first visit to Wilpattu with Paddy and Harry Maitland. Harry was an executive in the Mercantile Bank in Colombo and Paddy, his wife, was an accomplished artist. I had invited a young nursing sister from The Joseph Fraser Nursing Home in Colombo to come with us to make up a four. I met this same girl, then married, about thirty-five years later in the Sydney Opera House and it was clever of her to recognise the grey-haired old man who, so many years ago, had enticed her into the jungles of Ceylon. Anyway, we hired a jeep and set off for Wilpattu and arrived at the entrance to the reserve about lunch-time. Here we took our mandatory tracker on board and made our way to the wooden house in the jungle that was to be our home for the next few days. The house was sparsely furnished but spotlessly clean and the cook and other servants did their stuff admirably. After lunch we all had a siesta, because the animals do too, and set off in the evening on our first patrol. Wilpattu has many tanks within its boundaries – a tank is a large freshwater lake usually about ten or fifteen acres in size – and these tanks give homes to many species of bird – duck, teal, pelicans, flamingos and storks, herons and egrets of every imaginable variety. The tanks are full of fish and one particular variety – the lula is simply delicious when crumbed and fried and sprinkled with the juice of a fresh lime. All sorts of animals come to the tanks to drink, especially in the dry weather when their water-holes have turned into mud-holes.

Driving along the jungle tracks is fun too because one never knows what one might see round the next corner. Wilpattu has elephant, leopard, bear, boar, buffalo, red and spotted deer and, of course, snakes of all varieties. Monkeys abound from the black-faced wanderoo to the small 'widows' peak' monkey and, apart from the bird life I've already mentioned, there are jungle-fowl, pea fowl, hawks, kites, eagles and in the smaller varieties, drongos, minivets, sunbirds, kingfishers, babblers and many many others. Nasties like ticks, fleas, mosquitoes, scorpions, cockroaches, centipedes, etc, etc, are in good supply but I've never seen a leech in either Wilpattu or Yala. I've had many encounters with leeches, however, and I'll tell you about these later on.

On this particular visit we had a scare – it was early evening and we were well concealed in the undergrowth watching about eight or ten elephants, with some babies, splashing about in the shallows of a tank. We had our cameras out and a groundsheet and thermos flasks, etc and the elephants, about 100 yards away, gave no indication that they were aware of our presence. Suddenly the tracker became very agitated and said we must leave everything and walk quickly, not run, to the jeep. As we started to move an elephant trumpeted some twenty or thirty yards away to our flank. We got away and stayed away for about an hour and then went back cautiously and very quietly to get our things. The elephants were still splashing around and we watched for another ten minutes or so. Once again the tracker got worried and said we must go at once but to take all our things because we were not coming back. Again, as we left, the same 'sentry' elephant trumpeted and this time we heard him crashing through the jungle. We didn't hang about. A friend told me later that this was quite normal and that when a herd have babies with them a 'sentry' is posted to keep a look out. Our tracker called the sentry 'Uncle'!

We did not see leopard on that occasion but saw most other things. One can, under permit, take a gun into the reserve for self-protection but I never have. We shall be returning to Wilpattu and Yala for further visits later on.

About 1937 one of my friends, Gordon Armstrong, was given a small aeroplane, called a Flying Flea by his father. This was a single-seater affair propelled by a small aero-engine mounted on four stanchions above the pilot's head. The whole thing looked not unlike a flying bedstead because it had no fabric covering the air-frame and I was told it was dangerous to fly; dangerous because at low speeds, in certain circumstances, if one banked too steeply the overhead engine acted like a keel, turned the aeroplane upside down and the pilot was in difficulties trying to right it before landing. Gordon's parents heard about this and told him that if he would agree to destroy it (on the ground!) they would buy him something else. The

54

'something else' was a Taylor Cub, an American high-winged cabin monoplane, which held two and as far as I can remember, it had dual-controls. In fact, it must have done because I know we used to fly it all over the place.

This was the aeroplane in which Gordon nearly killed us both on two occasions. The trouble was that we could not afford high-octane aviation spirit and so we used to fly the Cub on the equivalent of our 4-star petrol and this meant we lost a lot of revs – ie power.

The first time we nearly met our Maker was in the very early days of the Cub. Gordon and I were not going anywhere in particular – we were just going to have an hour or so fooling around with Gordon practising the few minor aerobatics the Cub would allow. We started our take-off, into wind, along the grass of the aerodrome and being a bit low on power, with two people up, the Cub took some time to get unstuck from the ground. When Gordon did manage to lift her off our speed could not have been much more than 60 mph or so. It follows that the Cub was climbing very slowly and a line of palm trees was approaching very quickly. It was obvious we were not going to clear the trees and, instead of flying into them, Gordon did the only other thing possible – he did a down-wind turn. Let me explain – if an aeroplane is climbing with barely enough flying speed it means it is not far off stalling and if you attempt to turn it at such a time, down-wind, you lower the 'lift' of the wings and the aeroplane invariably spins into the ground with fatal results. The throttle was, of course, wide open and, having turned, Gordon dived the Cub towards the ground as hard as he could – he didn't have any great height in hand – say sixty or seventy feet – but he managed to get some flying speed again and levelled out about three feet from the grass. We went into the flying club bar and had a restorative or two.

The second occasion was at a place called Bentota. Now Gordon's father owned a small island called Barbaryn only a mile or so from Bentota and say half a mile from the mainland. I've spent many a hysterical weekend on that island but more of that anon – perhaps. Anyway, we had flown down to

Bentota, some thirty-five miles south of Colombo on the west coast of the island, for a weekend at Barbaryn. We landed on the beach at Bentota, a sort of long sandy peninsular, roped and pegged the Cub down, took out our miniscule suitcases and waited for Gordon's father to collect us in his motor-boat. The locals on the Bentota beach were fascinated because none of them had ever seen an aeroplane at such close quarters before. It poured with rain all that night but we didn't give it a thought and had the usual very happy, and boozy weekend. On the Sunday evening we said goodbye to Gordon's parents and prepared to fly back to Colombo. As soon as we stepped out of the motor-boat we knew some excitement lay ahead because the sand was very very wet and soggy. Gordon said he would fly the Cub back and I most thankfully agreed – it was his aeroplane anyway and he was very much the more experienced pilot. We un-roped the Cub, got in, and she started up at once. Knowing that take-off was going to be hairy off the wet sand, Gordon taxied right down the peninsular to the Bentota Resthouse at the south end. We turned – not quite into wind because it was coming off the sea, and found we had nearly a mile of beach as our runway. Gordon was flying from the back seat and I was in front. Well, that was the longest mile I've ever travelled and one I never want to travel again. I can't remember the exact figures but let us assume the Cub normally took off at 60 or 65 mph. I had my own instruments in front of me and I watched the air-speed indicator crawl sluggishly to 50 mph to 55 mph to 60 mph and we both could feel the wet sand dragging us back. Gordon tried to pick the Cub up into the air at 60 mph. She *just* lifted for, say, twenty yards and flopped back. We reached 65 mph and tried again – by this time we were running out of beach – still she would not fly and so Gordon tried one last time. The Cub came unstuck and the small waves at the end of the sandy peninsular we were on shot under our wheels. She wallowed in the air like a fat duck and started to descend – I closed my eyes and hung on to the dashboard in front of me. Hitting the sea at 70 mph was not going to be funny. Gordon managed to hold the Cub level at say six feet above the sea and, without that wretched sand, she

56

slowly gained flying speed and I knew we had made it. I turned round to ask my dear friend what he thought he was doing but he looked so awful I refrained.

About this time I was having flying lessons from the Ratmalana Aero Club instructor, a man called Duncanson. He was a flight-lieutenant I think and a fine instructor. 'Dunc', as he was called, was a charming man, quietly spoken and modest and a brilliant pilot – he was also very patient. I say this because in my early days he would put me in the front seat of a Gypsy Moth and once we had taken off he would give me the OK to take over. He would sense that I was tense and strung up and he would make me fly on a dead-level, straight course for what seemed like hours on end – in fact I suppose ten minutes. When I finally got bored with this exercise I would relax and flop back in my seat. Dunc would spot this immediately, the intercom would click and he would say, 'At last – now we can do some flying!'

I remember once at an air pageant at Ratmalana, Dunc did the most marvellous flying I've every seen. A Gypsy Moth arrived taxying along in front of the crowd with a lone pilot in the front seat – it stopped, the pilot got out and walked away, leaving the propeller still turning slowly. Suddenly the propeller started going faster and faster and the aeroplane started moving forward. The crowd stared horrified as the 'empty' aeroplane gained speed and took off. How Dunc managed to sit so low in the back seat I can't imagine, but he was literally out of sight, and then he did the full range of aerobatics over our heads finally coming in to land *upside down*! He flew over the grass runway at 80 or 90 mph some ten feet from the ground – still upside down, climbed to 100 feet or so, righted the aeroplane and landed the right way up. The Moth then taxied towards us – still 'empty'! It was brilliant.

Poor Dunc – some time before I was ready to go solo – he got into financial difficulties and then his instructor's licence was on the verge of expiring and he had no chance of renewing it. He was going to give a lesson one morning and, although it was a perfect day for flying, he told his pupil to stay in the club and he would soon be back after seeing what the conditions were like aloft. He took off, climbed to 6,000 feet, opened the throttle wide and dived the Gypsy Moth into the sea at full speed just near Mount Lavinia. His body was washed up a few days later. We were all very sad.

To return to Gordon Armstrong and his father's island, Barbaryn, for a moment. One day Gordon and I were crossing from the island to Bentota beach in his father's motor-boat when the propeller shaft sheared and the propeller and the bit of broken shaft disappeared into the sea. 'Dad'll kill me for this,' Gordon muttered, 'That was his favourite prop.' The boat started filling with water through the now empty shaft-housing and whilst Gordon was trying to stem the leak I went over the side to see if I could find the missing propeller. The water was much deeper than I had thought and there was no sign of the propeller, which was bad enough, but what was much much worse, in my view, was that there was a riptide running between the island and the mainland and Gordon and the helpless boat were miles away (well, fifty yards) when I got to the surface. The mainland was closer than the island and I made for that but there was this strong current against me. I must have been in the water for half an hour and I thought more than once – in fact I could think of nothing else – that I had had it. However, I finally made the beach and Gordon did too so all was well.

My dear friend had one more go at cutting me off in my prime and this was on our way back to Colombo after competing in a hill-climb on an up-country tea estate. We had both rowed in a regatta on the Saturday afternoon and we left for Nuwara-Eliya, four and a half hours away, after a scratch dinner, got to the course and slept as best we could in the car. This was an MG Tiger – a two-litre affair which looked far more potent than it really was. However, it was quick enough for Gordon to win his class and after some celebrations at the Grand Hotel in Nuwara-Eliya we set off down the hill again for Colombo. By 'hill' I mean 6,100 feet down to sea level. We took it in turns driving home and Gordon took over for the last hour. By this time it was dark, it was pouring, we had the hood down and we were soaked to the skin. We were doing about 60 mph on a straight bit of road when I saw a corner coming – 'He's cutting it a bit fine,' I thought to myself and then I glanced at Gordon. He was fast asleep. '*Gordon*,' I yelled and stuck my elbow in his ribs. He came to with a jolt, slammed on the brakes, hauled on the outside handbrake and tried to get round. No way – we left the road doing about 40 mph down a twelve foot bank and into a paddy-field nose first. We had no seat-belts in those days. He, poor man, lost a lot of front teeth on the steering wheel and I broke my nose on the scuttle. We were *still* good friends even after that!

I was sharing a rather elegant flat with Gordon about this time and it was four storeys high. It belonged to his father and Gordon once had a birthday party there. After dinner a bus was laid on to take everyone to Mount Lavinia beach for a midnight swim. Can you imagine? All went well – well, fairly well – until we were on the way back and nearing home after our beach picnic. A young lady sitting next to me in the bus had been very noisy and boisterous – suddenly she went very quiet, very pale and passed out across my knees, but not before getting violently sick all over me. When we got back to the flat everyone got out – said sweetly, 'Good luck, Bayne, dear boy,' and set off for their cars to take their girl-friends home. Well, I was stuck with this unconscious girl and we were both, through no fault of mine, in the most evil-smelling state. So I did the only thing possible – I carried her up four soul-searing flights of stairs to our flat and put her to bed. What it was to be young.

Another little incident springs to mind – one evening I was having dinner with some friends, this time in a *three*-storeyed flat. There were about six or eight of us present – all young men and we finished dinner at about midnight which was not all that unusual. I should explain that it was a furnished flat and it contained, amongst the usual things, an upright piano. Some-one enquired if any of us played the piano – we all said, 'No' and so we had the most reasonable discussion as to why there should be a piano in the flat if nobody could play it. We tried to find a logical answer to our problem and, as you can imagine, this took some time – until about 3 am in fact – and I suppose we had a drink or two whilst we were arguing. We came to a decision – the piano must go – and the most obvious way to dispose of it, surely, was to sling it over the balcony. We drew lots as to who would do the slinging and who would go downstairs on to the pavement to watch (and hear) the piano arrive. I was one of the lucky ones and downstairs I went – on to the pavement – opposite the Galle Face Hotel. There were not many passers-by at that hour of the morning and my friends and I watched the others – three storeys up – struggling with the piano. Finally they got it on top of the balcony railing and gave it an almighty shove. It is just possible that you have neither seen nor heard a piano fall three storeys onto a very solid pavement – well – take it from me it's a most spectacular event and the last chords from that unhappy instrument combined with the splintering of wood and groaning of tortured metal had to be heard to be believed. The owners made us buy them a new one – how mean can one get?

Quite recently I recounted that story at a dinner party and it went down well – as did the piano! When I had finished an ex-Fleet Air-Arm pilot said quietly, 'I think I can beat that.' I told him no-one, but no-one, could even equal such an extravaganza let alone beat it but 'do carry on' I encouraged him. He did. It seems that once, when he was serving in an aircraft-carrier somewhere or other, the young officers in the ward-room got bored after lunch and wondered what they could do to amuse themselves. Their eyes fell on the Ward-room piano and a similar argument to mine took place and a similar solution was agreed. They sent for an artificer and told the wretched man to gather some of his mates, take the piano to the flight deck and place it on one of the steam catapults that were used to launch the aeroplanes from the carrier. 'When a full head of steam has been raised,' they told the man, 'and the piano firmly in place – send for us.' This was duly done and to the ribald cheers of the merry matelots the wretched instrument was flung hundreds of yards into the Indian ocean – or maybe it was the Pacific! I had to admit my story paled into insignificance compared to this one.

In case you are now under the impression that my life was simply a large bowl of cherries, let me disillusion you. I was still

60

working hard and earning an honest crust. I was not at all like a friend I had who once said to me, 'It's this getting up before breakfast and working between meals that gets me down.' Actually, when I first started my insurance work with old man Kitching, some of the aunts from Thornleigh sent me a little text in a red 'morocco' frame which read, 'When you're young, work faithfully for eight hours a day and don't worry – then, in time you'll become the boss, work twelve hours a day and have all the worry.' Most encouraging.

By this time the old square-nosed Morris Oxford had been condemned as unfit to go on the road and I was given the most awful little Austin 7 tourer instead. This was quite the most unstable vehicle it was ever my misfortune to drive and it was not long before I wrote it off. (I have a son who would have done it even quicker.) This was the way of it – I was going back to the office after lunch one day when I saw a friend of mine – one Ian Munro – Reuters' man in Colombo – some way ahead of me in his MG. I thought I'd give him the shock of his life by passing his very smart red midget in my ancient bone-shaker. Accordingly I started to cram on as many revs as I could and began to close the distance between us. Suddenly, to my horror, some idiot coming the other way did a U-turn just in front of me and hit me full amidships. The Austin 7 rolled over about three times and came to rest on its hood with, I imagine its wheels spinning merrily in the air. I had already left the vehicle, through the windscreen, sometime during its gyrations and did myself quite a lot of no good. A passing motorist took me to hospital and this is where the really nasty bit began. A pair of sweet old nursing nuns took me in hand and clucked away saying over and over again, 'Oh you poor boy.' How kind, I thought, but changed my mind very smartly when one of them approached me with an open cut-throat razor in her hand. You see, I'd cut my right hand rather badly and a large lump of flesh was hanging off. I thought, 'Oh no! she's going to cut if off,' but all was well – she merely gently shaved the hairs away before stitching it up. They rang my father who came and collected me and I was put to bed. When my father came home from the office that evening he tossed the evening paper on to my bed and there was a photograph of the car on the front page. Concussion does funny things to a chap because, although I went to the wreckage after the accident and took out my topee and papers, I had not realised the car was upside down!

As I said earlier on, Jack Reeves was a keen oarsman and cox and I, having been to the Colombo Rowing Club and watched him, thought I would like to have a go. The club was situated right in the middle of Colombo and on the south-eastern bank of the Beira Lake. This was a stretch of fresh water with one or two canal outlets to the harbour. A one mile dog-leg provided a very good course for our regattas and, in the heat and humidity of Colombo, a mile race was quite long enough. To give you an example of what I mean – most of us were six or seven pounds lighter when we stepped out of the boat after rowing a course. We put it all back, however, by the time we left the boathouse having had our drinks. These were usually stout and tonics in half-pint tankards served by the boathouse stewards. The drill was that after getting out of the boat we went upstairs and took off our sopping wet rowing things and seized two large towels – one of these was wrapped round the waist, sarong style, and the other was draped fetchingly over the shoulders. The crew, either four or two, then sat on the lawn and enjoyed their much deserved drinks before going upstairs again for showers and changing into blazers and flannels. We had a lovely green lawn leading down to the lake and a feature was a pair of travellers' palms which had unique fan-shaped leaves and this was our crest. One stood at each end of the landing stage and they were much admired on regatta days by our guests.

Tradition has it that if one breaks off a palm frond there is water at the base of the stem and this will save a parched traveller's life. I've tried it and there *was* a dribble of water in the stem. It was the drowned spiders, flies and other nasties that I objected to. As I have said, the Beira Lake was more or less in the middle of the business sector of Colombo, some five minutes' drive from most offices and it was a most wonderful peaceful and tranquil change from the bustle and noise of the city.

Jack Reeves proposed me for membership and another friend – I forget who – seconded me and in due course I was summoned to meet the Committee. I was, I suppose, about twenty-two or twenty-three years old at this time and I will never forget that evening. I arrived at 5.30 pm at the boat-house as instructed, properly dressed with coat, tie – the lot. Our boathouse was a long building and housed all the boats, fours, pairs and sculling boats on the ground floor. Upstairs we had our locker room and showers, our bar and lounge and then at the far, or south, end was another large sitting-out area screened by potted palms from the bar and lounge. To this I was directed and the captain explained that most members of the committee were about to go out on the lake and they would see me in due course. Well, I waited and waited and waited. The committee had their row, had their drinks (as described) had their showers and changed and ordered their whiskies at the bar. At about 7.30 pm they sent for me, examined me, questioned me and said I could go and I would be hearing from the secretary in due course. They stood there drinking and I was not offered a thing. I later became captain and then president and the first thing I altered was the way in which candidates for election were received and welcomed.

I loved my rowing and met with a certain amount of success during the earlier part of the thirty odd years I was a member of the club. I will come back from time to time on rowing matters but there's just one rather sad incident I'll tell you about now.

Every year the Colombo Rowing Club would row against the Madras Rowing Club – one year in Colombo, the next in Madras. I was lucky enough to get selected for the Colombo crew and I was rowing at two in the boat. Our coach was one of the nicest of men, called Comrade Sutherland, and he used to take us out two or three times a week. A week or two before the big race Comrade had us out on the lake and he was disgusted with our performance. 'You're an idle lot of so-and-so's,' he yelled and, 'I want you all here at 6 am tomorrow before you go to the office!' Well, that evening he took his wife Audrie and a planter's wife to our Queen's Club for a drink or

63

two before going home for dinner. Having had their drinks the three of them were walking to their car when Comrade exclaimed that he had been bitten by something. They got a torch from the car and examined Comrade's ankle and there were two little red dots. In case it was a snake, they drove to a small nursing home nearby where the most brillaint surgeon named Spittle was the owner. Unforunately, Spittle was away but the matron said she suspected it *was* a snake bite and she was going to admit Comrade there and then for treatment and observation. Comrade protested violently and said in no way was he going to be admitted and, he added, as a most illogical afterthought, 'Anyway, I haven't had dinner yet!' After some argument Comrade had his way but he promised he would come back if he felt ill in the night. He died in the early hours of the morning. So instead of rowing in the morning the whole crew went to Comrade's funeral that evening.

Another snake story – one of my partners in the office called Mac Bartlett had a son, Michael, aged eight or nine and one Sunday morning, like so many other small boys, he was climbing a tree in the garden. Suddenly he came rushing into the house yelling that he had been bitten by a snake. His father bundled young Michael into the car having first told Sally, his wife, to telephone the Joseph Fraser Nursing Home to say that they were on their way and would they please arrange for a Buddhist priest to be there as quickly as he could. I should explain that a number of Buddhist priests very skilfully prepared and kept anti-snake bite serums which have saved many lives. I think the ayurvedic ingredients they used have been handed down over the generations but one ingredient is certainly snake venom.

Well, the Buddhist priest arrived soon after Michael and his father reached the nursing home and Michael was closely questioned by the priest so that the specie of snake could be identified if possible. After a little while the priest took Mac Bartlett into a private room and said, 'I think your son has made up this story and I don't believe he has been bitten by a snake at all. I think a tree rat has bitten him.' (A tree rat is a breed of a rather miserable mangy-looking squirrel we have in

64

Ceylon.) So Mac said it didn't matter, surely, if Michael had been bitten by a snake or not – inject him anyway. The priest said, 'If Michael has been bitten by a snake the injection I give him will do him good – if he has not been bitten by a snake, it will kill him – what do you want me to do?' Poor Mac, what a quandary! He took Michael aside and explained that he quite understood that small boys made up heroic stories and imagined things but this was very serious and please, *please* was it a snake? Michael, in tears, said he *saw* the snake – it was *not* a tree rat and it was a *snake* that had bitten him. So Mac had to come to a most ghastly decision – he went to the priest and said, 'Inject him.' It *was* a snake and Michael is still alive and kicking.

Some time before this I had the excitement of buying my first car. This was an MG 18/80 and although it was second-hand it had been beautifully kept and carefully used by the original owner. He was a man called Francis Whittaker and he was Secretary to the Ceylon Chamber of Commerce for many years. He had a dashing, desperado look about him because he wore a black patch over one eye. The MG was a lovely car – only slightly shorter than a three litre Bentley and with the most elegant lines. The open body was black fabric leather, by Weymann, the bonnet black steel and the long sloping front mudguards and the leather upholstery were emerald green. Very smart she was and I was desperately proud of her and used to swank a lot. A particular feature was an outside handbrake and I used to use this a lot just for showing off purposes. The MG was similar to Gordon Armstrong's but not quite so fast and less flashy and I competed in many hill-climbs with her with varying degrees of success.

I was competing once in a hill-climb in Nuwara Eliya on a tea estate called Mahagastotte and, as usual, all the drivers forgathered in the Grand Hotel that evening for drinks and dinner before leaving for Colombo or elsewhere. I was just getting ready to leave when a very pretty Colombo girl with auburn hair came and asked me whether I could give her a lift home. I knew her slightly and had always admired her but we seemed to move in different circles. I was alone, there was an empty passenger seat, it was a beautiful moonlit night so, in about ten seconds flat, I was settling her down in the MG and wrapping her up with spare sweaters and anything else I could lay my hands on. Six thousand feet at night in an open car can be quite chilly and I was most anxious to make a good impression on my delectable passenger. As we started off, some words my father had said to me more than once came to mind – 'If you ever have an accident and hurt yourself, your mother and I will be very sad and upset but if you ever so much as hurt a hair of your passenger's head I'll never speak to you again.' Stern words and he probably didn't really mean them but they sank in and I have never forgotten them. My sons have had the same treatment.

Anyway, all went well and four and a half hours later I deposited my young passenger with, I think, a large chunk of my heart, on her parents' doorstep in Colombo. We saw a lot of each other over the next few months – parties, visiting planting friends, dinner-dances – the usual things – and only once did I fall foul of her father. We had been swimming at Mount Lavinia after some party or other and we started for home about midnight. Like a clot, whilst reversing the MG on a very narrow track near the beach I put a back wheel into a ditch. Everyone else had gone and she was a big car. With herself at the wheel and me trying to pick up the back of the car, we struggled and struggled for about two hours. Finally we got the car out and we arrived at the parental home about 3 am. 'Father' was waiting – he was unamused and he let me have it, 'Where the devil, etc.' He carried on for about five minutes. At last he calmed down and when he saw his daughter was safe and sound he became quite civil. When he saw the state of my clothes and with my hands covered in blood, mud, grease, etc, he forgave all and even offered me a drink!

This same young lady – nameless you notice – was very attractive, as I've said, and I was very fond of her indeed. She must have been fond of me too because one evening something quite unusual happened. We were sitting in the MG, it might well have been in her drive before I saw her into her house, – when she turned to me and said, 'Will you marry me?' I think

66

I've never been so startled but, at the same time, I was terribly pleased, flattered and I felt most honoured. I explained very gently that there was nothing I'd love more but I was simply in no position to marry. I was twenty-five, doing quite well but certainly not well enough to entertain any thoughts of marriage. She replied that if it was a lack of funds that was worrying me there was no problem. 'My father,' she said, 'will give you a job good enough to let you marry me and for us to live quite comfortably.' It was very very hard for me to stick to my principles but I simply had to and I explained, again as gently as I could, why I was not yet ready to marry.

To say I was upset conveys nothing – I was utterly miserable but only for two days or so because, you see, two days after our little discussion in the car her engagement was announced to an assistant superintendent of Police! I didn't even know there *was* another man involved so my little friend was a good actress. I still missed her and thought of her a lot for many months and I must have been very much in love because I could never think ill of the wretched child!

6

1937 – 1938
My First Leave

About this time my first leave was due after seven years in Colombo. Old Kitching was not the most generous of employers! In those days a five year first contract was the norm and for the more senior people, three years. Then again, the more junior one was the more rotten season one got for one's leave. I was given October to March but still, six months holiday on full pay was a thrilling prospect and as October 1937 approached the more excited I got. We had one or two quite good stores in Colombo where one could get a reasonably made suit cut by an English tailor. I bought two, plus a camel hair overcoat which were all the rage in those days. I still have that overcoat and still wear it on shabby occasions but, after fifty-five years service, it must have been very good value.

In addition to full pay one was given a first-class return passage to London and we all thought that the three weeks' voyage there and the three weeks back were the highlights of one's leave because one lived practically free. Whisky was tuppence a glass on board, and gin and beer were about the same – say – under a penny today!

The ship I sailed on was the P & O *Mooltan* and she had started her voyage at Calcutta I think. Anyway, there was a very nice chap on board from a Calcutta bank called Felix Hill and he and I spent a lot of our leave together. We shared the same digs in North London and the first thing we did was to buy ourselves a car each. Mine was a new MG Midget and I took delivery from the factory in Abingdon. I remember the day well – it was bright and sunny and there was this super little green car with its hood down and a man in a brown overall going over it with a yellow duster. I gave him half-a-crown. Felix was more sedate and bought himself an Austin 12 Saloon. The strange thing was that he couldn't drive a car and so we took turns as to which car we would use and I did all the driving.

To return to the *Mooltan* and the voyage to England – this was my first leave in seven years and very exciting it was too. I shall never forget the thrill of the first few mornings at sea – one's steward brought in one's early morning tea, biscuits and fruit and then I went for a swim before breakfast. The swimming pool was primitive, to say the least, in those days because it consisted of a large tarpaulin slung between some derricks and filled with sea-water. One had to be careful about sticking one's head under the water because in the heat from Colombo to Aden and then up the Red Sea the pool water evaporated very quickly and the pool was then topped up with more sea-water so the concentration of salt was severe and ear-ache was commonplace.

After my swim I would make my way to the dining-saloon for breakfast – a modest affair of fruit juice, bacon and eggs, toast marmalade and coffee and then – joy of joys – up on deck and no work – no peons – no telephones just idleness on a beautiful blue sea waiting for the bar to open.

Felix Hill and I soon made friends with each other and then we made friends with other people on board. These were the days when one was young and naive and made friends from the first day at sea. More often than not this was not a good idea because invariably one met the wrong sort of people and got stuck with them for the rest of the voyage. Particularly I have in mind a young divorcee to whom on a much later leave I had an introduction from an elderly dragon-like lady I knew in Colombo. I was having a drink before lunch on the first day at sea and I asked the steward casually if he knew a Mrs so-and-so. He said yes he did and so I asked him merely to point her out sometime so that I could have a look before introducing myself. To my alarm he was back in less than a minute with the lady in question and presented her to me. I offered her a drink and explained who I was. She had a drink, and then another and then another and it was plain she was an alcoholic. Two evenings later it was the ship's fancy-dress dinner and dance and, naturally, I declined to have any part of this and went down to dinner in my dinner-jacket as usual. As I was about to leave the table this dreaded girl came up to me, explained she was going to the dance as a brown paper parcel and would I please pin her up! Well, I'd had a good dinner but she had had a very very good dinner and I wondered with some interest what would happen when we reached her cabin. I didn't have long to wait. She produced yards and yards of brown paper and a box of large pins and told me to get cracking. I need hardly say I'd never pinned a girl into a brown paper parcel in my life before and she was fairly caustic at the way in which I started. It was only when I drove a large pin into her ribs that she let me have it. I had never heard such language from any female before (I never want to again) but she screamed and yelled and, I thought, she was on the verge of apoplexy. 'You'd better send for your stewardess,' I said and departed much shaken. This was a lesson I never forgot and ever since I've made it a golden rule never to talk to strange passengers at least until we've reached Aden.

There were *some* nice people on board the *Mooltan* particularly one charming girl called Bunty Bisseker who had had a holiday in India and was on her way home. Bunty's parents lived in Cambridge where her father, the Reverend Bisseker, had been Headmaster of Leys School. They were the most charming and gentle couple and Felix and I spent a few days on two occasions with them at their home in the village of Harston just outside Cambridge. They were kindness itself and spoilt us in the most generous way. Felix and I were warned on one occasion to bring white ties with us, which we did and attended, thus attired, our first May Week Ball. My leave must have been December to May and not as I said earlier on because it was certainly May Week when Felix and I were in Cambridge. I remember there were about six of us in a punt on the Cam, as the sun came up and it was all great fun. I watched some of the May Week rowing too and some of the rugger crews had to be seen to be believed – they were obviously better at rugger than they were at rowing.

Bunty later married a most handsome young parson called Oswald Sills and he was attached to Ely Cathedral. His particular function was that of Fabric Officer which meant that he had to carry out regular inspections of the cathedral to look for damp, rot, weather damage, etc. One morning at breakfast Oswald asked me if I was any good at heights and I replied that, as far as I knew, heights didn't worry me and what had he got in mind? He said it was his morning to inspect the inside of the Octagon and would I like to go along. 'Of course,' I said and off we went. We started at the west end of the marvellous old building and immediately started climbing innumerable stone staircases. Eventually we emerged into the simply vast enclosure which was the nave or main part of the cathedral. We were some eighty feet up I suppose, although it felt much higher, and the visitors on the ground looked like ants. We were facing east and looking towards the choir stalls and altar and the simply enormous stained glass windows that ran north to south across the whole width of Ely Cathedral. We were standing on an eighteen inch ledge which had a metal railing and, if I remember correctly, this came to knee level only. Oswald led the way and I followed and every now and then he'd stop and look up to see if all was well above our heads. I found this exercise hard to do and I seemed to be forming a fascinating and possibly fatal attraction for the very hard and cold floor eighty or ninety feet below. We minced along going east and, had I known it at the time, this was the easy bit. I say this because having gone for what seemed like miles over the chancel and choir stalls and above the main altar our little ledge did two things. First it turned left, or north and then, horrors, the little railing stopped. So there we were, say eighty feet up on an eighteen inch ledge – no railing – people like ants below – and stained glass windows going say, another thirty or forty feet above our heads. I discovered at once I was *not* good at heights and I told Oswald without

71

further delay that all was not well with me. He was very calm and said, 'Oh dear!' Very helpful. I had the awful feeling of being marooned – no way forward, no way back – I was simply stuck! Oswald said over his shoulder, 'Turn sideways and face down the cathedral but don't look down whatever you do. Now press your hands firmly against the stained glass window behind you and walk sideways like a crab, leaning back as much as you can.' Well, I covered that fifty yards or so, fighting back the all-consuming desire to fall forwards, and eventually reached the north wall where our ledge turned west and where the little railing started again. Finally we reached ground level again and I've never been so thankful for *terra firma*. We then went up the Octagon – twice the height of the cathedral roof – but this didn't worry me a bit because we were enclosed and there was always something to hang on to. Oswald told me that the oak beams in the octagon – say twenty-four or thirty-six inches square – simply vast – were carried over the River Cam by oxen-drawn carts in the eleventh century. How building construction people in those days managed without today's modern cranes and other mechanical aids to lift vast pieces of masonry and colossal balks of wood to great heights – I will never know. I rather 'went off' Oswald Sills for a bit after that morning! Poor Oswald – he died a year or two ago and so Bunty was all alone, poor dear, for many years.

There was another awfully nice elderly couple on board the *Mooltan* and it was Bunty who introduced me to them. They were a Mr and Mrs Raphael and they were coming home after a holiday and they were accompanied by their young niece, Dora Flinders, known, of course, as 'Polly'. I used to spend hours chatting to the Raphaels because, although they were much older than I was, they were much travelled and could talk on about any subject or country in the world. They lived in Newmarket and, as you might suspect, their great love was racing. They once asked Felix and me to stay and, once again having been warned to bring our tails, we left London in my little MG and set off for Newmarket. We arrived at teatime and we had the shock of our lives because at the top of the front steps to greet us was a butler. 'Leave the car and your luggage, sir,' he said, 'the footmen will see to all that – I'll show you to your rooms and Madam is waiting for you in the drawing-room.' After tea we went back to our rooms to unpack but, as we should have guessed, this had already been done. Poor Felix – he was in a great state because his tails were fresh that morning from Moss Bros and he was horrified at what our valet must have thought. One further surprise awaited me when I crawled into bed – the sheets were silk – never have I had such luxury. Our few days with the Raphaels were simply marvellous – never had I lived in such style and they were kindness itself. We had, after all, only met on a boat but they treated Felix and me as if we had known each other all our lives.

I don't like telling lies but one day at the Raphaels I had to. Mrs Raphael had given Felix and me their badges and tickets to the enclosure at Newmarket and sent us off for an afternoon at the races. Before we left Mrs R. asked me if I had done much racing in England and I confessed I had never been to the races anywhere in the world and this seemed to be exactly the answer she wanted. 'Here are some good horses for you, Alan,' she said and handed me a slip of paper which I put in my pocket and to which I never gave another thought. Felix and I had a good time, had a drink or two and lost a lot of money. On arriving back Mrs R. was beaming and told me delightedly how glad she was that every horse she had given me was a winner. I remembered, at last, that wretched bit of paper in my pocket which I hadn't even looked at. Here comes the lie – 'I can't thank you enough,' I said, 'I've made so much more money than I expected to and I'm more than grateful.' Not making any money was bad enough but deceiving dear old Mrs R. made me feel simply dreadful.

During this leave Felix and I met two very nice girls – I don't remember how – their name was Wilcox although they were not related and one was Norah and the other Helen. They worked in a beauty parlour in Bond Street called The Powder Box and they were very good value. Just before my leave ended I took Helen to a ball in London – it must have been something pretty grand because I was in white tie and tails and felt very self-conscious in the MG with the hood down in broad daylight driving through London.

After the party I dropped Helen back at her flat in Streatham and I must have had a pretty good evening because the next thing I remember was waking up in a stable yard in Paddington – still in an open MG, still in tails and with the spring sun shining down on me. My navigation must have gone adrift somewhere.

An uneventful voyage back to Colombo followed and back to the grindstone I went. My new agreement with Kitching was to be for four years but the war in 1939 intervened and so I didn't see England again until 1947.

7

1938 – 1944
The War Years and the One-Eyed Soldier

From the time I got back to Colombo in 1938 until the outbreak of war in September 1939 I lived with my parents and Phyllys, my sister, in a brand new house. A very rich Greek (aren't they all!) called Harry Cosmos had bought himself a large plot of land in the Cinnamon Gardens area of Colombo and he built six very nice detached houses on it. The plot of land was off Barnes Place and Cosmos called his little lane Marina Avenue and each of the six houses was named after a Greek island. Ours was called Leros and the others were Delos, Naxos, Paros, etc. They were well-made, large and airy, and we were very comfortable there. My quarters were on the ground floor and the others lived upstairs. My bathroom had a sunken bath and some rather saucy murals of naked women were painted on the walls. I felt no pain.

I had planned to go up-country one weekend and on Saturday 2 September 1939 I was shaving before my shower and my boy was packing for me. Suddenly my father appeared – 'And where do you think you're going?' he asked – I said he knew I was going up-country for the weekend. 'Not any more,' he said 'We're mobilized – into uniform and I'll drive you to headquarters.' It was quite a shock and I found it hard to believe that my whole life was going to change quite substantially from that moment on. My mother was detailed off to phone my up-country friends and my father and I reported for duty. I was put into a section of seven men and we were posted to the end of the Colombo Harbour breakwater, with rifles and a Lewis gun, to sink the German Navy if it appeared! Of course nothing happened and my section was relieved and replaced by another one some hours later. The following day, 3 September 1939, war was declared and a number of German nationals were rounded up and put into rather gentle and civilized concentration camps. One couple were my sister's friends and she thought nothing of the idea. 'Quite ridiculous and unnecessary,' she said. In the event nothing happened in the eastern hemisphere and after a few weeks we were demobilized again and we returned to our civilian activities.

I thought this would be a good time to leave the 'Stout and Tonics' and transfer to the Ceylon Planters' Rifle Corp. My CO was not amused but, as my father knew him well in civilian life, he agreed. So I became Rifleman Bayne in due course and never for a moment regretted the transfer.

Although we, in Colombo, had been demobilized temporarily in October 1939, war was a very real matter in the west, and France and England were having a very nasty time. Because India had fought so wonderfully well for Great Britain in the 1914/18 war, along with so many other nations, Army Headquarters in Delhi decided to start recruiting officers and men as there was no doubt that they were going to be needed once again. Accordingly, Base Area in Colombo was ordered by Delhi to start calling for volunteers to attend Officer training schools in India. I suppose it was early in 1940 that Ceylon started getting together the first contingent to go to India. Volunteers were called for and I told old Kitching I was off and would he please look after my insurance agency for the duration. I reported to CPRC Headquarters and was sent off to RAMC HQ for my medical. All went well until it came to the matter of sight and the chief medico, one Major Sheppard RAMC, said 'Read that board with your right eye.' I did so, 'Now your left eye,' 'I can't,' I said, 'I'm blind in my left eye.' 'I'll have to turn you down,' said Major Sheppard. I pleaded, I cajoled. I told him I had been an efficient volunteer soldier for six or seven years. I said having only one eye hadn't hindered me in life at all for twenty-seven years. I added that having one eye hadn't hindered Nelson. He was adamant.

A few months later, Delhi called for a second contingent and another fifty or sixty of my friends all volunteered – so did I and the same thing happened – (old man Kitching started getting a bit fed up with me) and I went back to the office very disappointed. Early in 1941 they called for a third contingent – off I went again and once more I had the same pantomime with Major Sheppard, with the same result. This time I lost my temper and told Sheppard his attitude was ridiculous and that surely some regiment could find some use for me. He said, 'Be reasonable, Bayne, supposing you were leading a platoon or a company into battle and you were shot through your good eye, what would you do?' 'I'd drop dead like anyone else I suppose,' I said. 'Don't be impertinent,' said Sheppard. I left. About two years later I recounted this story to my regimental sergeant-major, a Royal Welsh Fusilier and a most splendid man. 'I wish I'd known you was going for that medical, sir,' he said. 'Why?' I asked. 'I'd have got you through,' he said. 'How?' I asked. 'Well, sir, when the major asks you to read the letters with your right eye, you puts your *right* hand over your left eye – then when he says to read with your left eye you puts your *left* hand over your *left* eye. It works every time, sir.' I wish he *had* been there to tell me at the time.

So that was that, or so it appeared, and back I went to my little insurance agency. Nothing very exciting happened and selling insurance seemed very tame compared to what my friends were doing in Belgaum, Bangalore, Quetta and other OTCs in India. One friend was particularly lucky – he was Charles Cameron and he was posted directly to the training depot of the Cameron Highlanders.

Had I but known it, I was not going to sell many more insurance policies. In 1942 Japan bombed Pearl Harbour and, at last, the war was likely to reach the eastern hemisphere. This was quite a different kettle of fish and the CPRC mobilized every one they could. Both battalions were sent to Diyatalawa, which, as you know, is in the hills some four or five hours' drive from Colombo. This was not the usual jolly annual camp – this was serious and Rifleman Bayne – the one-eyed soldier – finally left his insurance business in the hands of Mr Kitching (on very generous terms for him, I might add) until I came back at some unknown date.

I was posted to Headquarters Company of the Colombo Battalion and my CO was a Major Gilliatt who in civilian life was an up-country tea-planter. He was known to his friends as Squirrel and he had been in a Highland Regiment in the First World War – I'm not quite sure which regiment but on occasions he used to wear his Glengarry (irregularly, I believe) with his CPRC uniform and very dashing he looked.

I seemed to have a flair for dismantling a Bren gun and re-assembling it without having any spare parts left over at the end of the operation. So I was given a stripe and put in charge of a section: a 'command' at last even if it was pretty humble. It had its funny moments too because some of the men in my section were senior to me in civilian life.

We had a team of PSI's (Permanent Staff Instructors) overlooking us and they were 'regular' warrant officers from various British regiments. Jack Grindley, later to be my RSM, was one of them.

We paraded, did a lot of drilling, had night exercises once or twice a week and generally became very fit. There was much healthy rivalry between the planters and the Colombo wallahs but this was always friendly. Our living conditions were pretty good too – we had the long corrugated iron huts I've mentioned previously, with cement floors and they must have been heated at nights but I can't remember how. The food was plain but good and there was always plenty of it. I missed not having my boy with me and found laying out my own uniform was very boring.

One morning a sergeant annoyed me and I only mention the incident because of the speed at which retribution struck him. He was a planter and a nasty bit of work and the coolies on his tea estate must have been delighted when he was mobilized. Anyway, I was taking my section off to PT early one morning when we met Sergeant X of the CPRC. 'Corporal,' he yelled, 'what are you doing?' 'I'm taking my section to PT, sergeant,

I replied. 'Well double, you idle lot – there's a war on!' he shouted. As I say, I was unamused. Later on that morning I was teaching my section how to take a Bren to pieces and re-assemble it when an orderly from headquarters came up and told me that Major Gilliatt, the company commander, wanted to see me. I left the senior rifleman in charge and went off suspecting that Sergeant X hadn't cared for my manner earlier that day and had reported me. I was taken in to the CO's office by the Orderly sergeant. I stood to attention and saluted. 'Sit down, Corporal Bayne,' said Squirrel Gilliatt. Much to my surprise I sat down and wondered what on earth was coming. Major Gilliatt said, 'You've got a good record, Corporal Bayne, and I understand you were a CSM (Company Sergeant Major) in the Stout & Tonics before you transferred to us, is that so?' 'Yes, Sir,' I answered. 'Well, I'm short of a CSM in Headquarters' Company. Would you like to have a go?' asked the good Major. 'Yes, Sir, I would,' I replied. 'Good,' said Major G. 'Go to Mr Clazey, the RSM and draw your fried egg and you'll be expected in the warrant officers' mess for lunch.' I should explain that a 'fried egg' was army slang for the badge of rank that a CSM wore on his wrist when he was wearing a short-sleeved shirt. The badge looked not unlike a brass fried egg and off I went and collected it. Next, I walked round the camp looking for Sergeant X. I saw him before he saw me and he was a little distance away. 'Sergeant,' I yelled. He turned round and saw it was me. 'Come here, Sergeant, I want to talk to you,' I called. I thought he was going to have a fit. He strolled up to me purple in the face. 'Never, in future, sergeant, reprimand an NCO in front of his men,' I said. Now I was *certain* he was going to have a fit. Then he saw my fried egg. To do him justice he collected himself very quickly – stood to attention and said, 'Sorry, sergeant-major.' Game, set and match I thought.

The great joy of being promoted to CSM was that I was entitled to a batman. This happy state of affairs lasted for about six months during which time we prepared ourselves for a possible confrontation with the Japanese. Having taken Singapore and made a start on Burma, it seemed logical they would try and move north-westwards to invade and capture Ceylon and India. There were other Ceylon Defence Force Units in Diyatalawa as well as us. There was for instance the Ceylon Light Infantry, a regiment of Ceylonese soldiers, Buddhist, Hindu, Muslim, C of E and Roman Catholic but, apart from the Regimental Commander and one Lt. Colonel who were English, they were all Asian. Good little soldiers they were too – I don't say 'little' disparagingly in any way – they *were* 'little' because their average height was about five foot five inches.

One day I was told that, for some weeks, the CPRC would take over guard duties of the camp from the CLI and would I make the necessary arrangements. First, I called on my opposite number in the CLI and made sure his drill for mounting and dismounting a regimental guard was the same as mine. Then I selected my first guard – they were all six foot three or more – Phil Fowke of 'leopard' fame was one of them and I drilled them until they were really very very smart. The big day arrived and a large number of spectators attended and it all went like clockwork and I was very impressed with my six foot plus gentlemen taking over from their 'little' five foot plus opposite numbers.

Route marches figured a lot in our weekly activities and on church parade mornings we borrowed the CLI band which always seemed to have a wonderful smartening-up effect on the brutal and licentious soldiery. We used a lot of live ammunition on the range and got used to our mortars, anti-tank weapons, grenades and three varieties of machine-gun – the Vickers, the Bren and the almost obsolete Lewis. At night we used tracers and this was always spectacular.

Towards the middle of 1942, Col Gilliatt sent for the RSM, his platoon commanders and me and told us that the Ceylon Light Infantry was short of officers and they wanted ten CPRC men to come over to them to boost morale. The ten who were selected would be commissioned at once, as captains, and would be posted as company commanders to the various CLI battalions.

We agreed on various people who all wanted commissions

and a change from Diyatalawa and eight people were selected from a short list. They were, Lawrence Harvey, Roy Webber, Harry Salter, Hamish Sinclair, Patrick Tremenheere, Murray Bremner, Jamie Robertson and me.

As I was the senior member of the party, I was put in charge until we reported to CLI headquarters in Colombo. We had a bit of a party at Diyatalawa before we caught the night mail to Colombo. As we were embarking, one of our number was so sloshed he walked into the carriage, opened the far door and fell out on to the tracks some four or five feet below, fortunately, for him, without serious injury.

The following morning I paraded my little party, still dressed as CPRC Riflemen, etc at CLI headquarters and reported to the adjutant. We were all given instructions and warrants for our uniforms and told to report to the various battalion headquarters to which we had been posted.

In the military section of the *Ceylon Government Gazette* we read that on that morning we had all been given commissions as second-lieutenants, promoted to lieutenants and finally promoted to captains all on the same morning.

I was posted to the 4th Battalion to take command of 'D' Company. I was just a little apprehensive. Here was I, a white man, ordered to take command of about 110 Ceylonese, officers, one warrant officer, NCO and men and I felt there might, quite reasonably, be some resentment. I went to my parents' house, had a bath and changed into my new uniform, complete with captain's pips, got into my car and drove off to Devon House, to the north of Colombo and close to the harbour, my first headquarters.

In the event I need not have worried. The company commander I was relieving met me and could not have been more welcoming. He showed me round, introduced me to the young subalterns and generally put me in the picture as to our duties.

I then called on my battalion commander who was a Lieutenant-Colonel Martenstyn who, in civilian life, was a senior executive in the Department of Customs and Excise. He was desperately proud of his battalion, was a strict disciplinarian and a man of high principles and even higher standards. I knew I was going to like him from our first meeting and I never had any reason to alter my initial assessment. He was a burgher, that is to say a mixture of either Dutch or Portuguese blood originally and whose ancestor married someone from Ceylon. Col Martenstyn's second-in-command was a Major Kumaranayagam, a full-blooded Tamil and, once again, a charming and efficient officer. To digress for a moment – some years after the war had ended and we were all back in our offices, Kumaranayagam came to see me one day. He asked me if I had ever thought about becoming a freemason. He went on to explain that initiation was strictly by invitation and that he and some others had been watching me for some time and felt I would be a suitable candidate. I told Kum that my father had been a keen mason and that I would think about it. Briefly, I was initiated, became master of my lodge after ten years or so and, although I no longer practice, I benefited from those years and I hope I helped other people too.

To return to 'D' Company – our main duty was to guard the north-western approaches to Colombo Harbour. My officers and I were billeted in a rambling old house and the men and their messes and our stores, etc had accommodation in our grounds which were extensive.

Gradually I got to know everyone in 'D' Company and the great majority were good soldiers and a very happy and cheerful lot. There was only one man who frightened me regularly – he was my personal driver and word got round that I used to race cars and enter up-country hill climb events. This character was always keen to show me what *he* could do and it was terrifying.

I suppose about fifty or sixty men were on guard duty at a time and so I always had about half the company available for training. I used to find my nightly rounds a little scary at times. I would go out at three or four in the morning to see how many sentries were asleep and I would creep up on them as quietly as I could. This was a hair-raising experience because their rifles were loaded and some were a little trigger-happy.

My second-in-command was a Lieutenant Kitto who, whilst

a bit 'bolshie' and self-opinionated, was the most marvellous sprinter and he used to win all the regimental sports events with great ease. Mostly, though, I was lucky in my company. Food was a slight problem in the officers' mess because curry was the order of the day before I arrived and, although I love it, I found curry more than once a day a bit much. We compromised and had eggs, etc for breakfast, curry for lunch and soup, middle course (sometimes goat!) and pudding for dinner. All very civilized.

(I am writing this bit in The Savoy where Moose and I are spending two nights. It's about fifty years later than the last paragraph and a good deal more pleasant.)

Back to Devon House – no real excitement during our, say, six months' stay, although there was a two weeks' training exercise which Base Area dreamed up for the battalion but it was 'D' Company who was detailed off to carry it out. A rubber estate thirty-one miles from our HQ was selected; it was called Usk Valley and a most charming elderly planter was in charge. I decided the company would march there and this shook Base Area, Battalion HQ and, of course 'D' Company who all thought I was quite mad. We set off at first light, were picked up by the CLI Band at about 9 am for a mile or two and reached our camp before dusk. I felt thirty-one miles with 110 men in one day, in daylight, was quite an achievement. We had the most awful monsoon rains after the first week in camp and the river just below us started rising alarmingly. At dusk I had pegs placed in the ground to the river's edge and ordered a picket guard to be mounted through the night and the guard commander had orders to call me when the rising river reached the last peg. This took place at about 3 am and my little bugler sounded the 'stand to' and we started to move. The river was literally following us as we moved, with hurricane lamps and a torch or two as our only illumination, and we reached the road at dawn. We moved our tents, equipment, arms and ammunition and ourselves in good order and the only casualty we suffered was one hockey ball and one rifle cleaning rod. The leeches had a field day. (The poem, 'Odd Flood Ode', at the end of the book may amuse you.)

At Devon House we had a heavy artillery battery stationed almost next door to us. I was told that it was suspected that their security was sloppy and Col Martenstyn asked me if I would care to test matters. I had an RAF friend called Peter Kershaw who was a Hurricane pilot and from him I borrowed an RAF hat, badges of rank, etc, etc. In my haversack I had six circular cigarette tins filled with sand and I drove up to the artillery battery gates. I was challenged by the sentry and I asked for the guard commander. I explained that I had a message for the battery second-in-command – Major X – and as it was top secret I could only deliver it to him. I was asked to wait and I remarked to the guard commander that I had never before seen such huge guns and such beautifully kept guns and could I have a look round whilst I was waiting. He agreed and off I went and surreptitiously placed a cigarette tin (supposed to be an explosive device) against the breech mechanism of each gun. I then told the guard commander I couldn't wait any longer and pushed off, phoned Col Martenstyn, told him what I had done and awaited developments. These were not long in coming and relations between the battery officers and me became somewhat strained. It was just as well perhaps that 'D' Company was transferred to Trincomalee soon after.

At Trincomalee we were stationed at the China Bay aerodrome and our duties were to guard the considerable area of the airfield and hangers. As far as I remember, the aeroplanes were Swordfish, (torpedo bombers) known affectionately as 'Stringbags', and I think some Beauforts, again torpedo bombers. It was a nice change from Devon House mainly because I could watch aeroplanes all day long. The RAF Officers were, as usual, very friendly and hospitable and I spent many a happy evening in their messes. Swimming was marvellous from long white sandy beaches and our rations improved no end because fish and shellfish were in plentiful supply. It was at China Bay I discovered the delights of arrack, a spirit distilled from the flower of the kitul palm, and to describe it I cannot do better than quote Noël Coward: 'It tasted simply filthy but with after effects divine.' Arrack's chief property, for me, was the lightning way in which it removed all traces of tiredness. Whisky and gin were severely rationed and I found that a shot of arrack after the day's work prepared one for more or less anything the evening had to offer.

I had a nasty shock one afternoon – a Royal Marine major called on me and asked me how many men I had, what weapons, transport, etc. Having decided he was 'real' and he was not up to some 'security' dodge I told him I had 110 men with the usual company arms of rifles, stens, two inch mortars, grenades and the officers had pistols. 'Why do you want to know this?' I asked. He told me that early that morning a Catalina flying boat, from a squadron at Koggala some eighty miles south of Colombo, had spotted a Japanese fleet of about fifty or sixty transport vessels, one or two aircraft-carriers and the usual escort of cruisers, destroyers, etc in the Indian Ocean heading towards Ceylon and some 300 or so miles from Trincomalee. 'How nice,' I said. The Catalina pilot had had just enough time to get off a frantic radio signal to our C in C in Colombo before he was shot down by Jap Zero fighters and taken prisoner with his crew.

The RM Major said we could expect a raid on China Bay aerodrome at first light in the morning and a possible invasion in strength somewhere along our east coast. The Trincomalee sector seemed the most likely place because of its most wonderful harbour, its good rail facilities and very good roads. Ceylon, of course, was the obvious place for the Japs to establish a bridgehead for an assault on India: only twenty-one miles of sea – the Palk Straits – separated India from Ceylon.

'What can we do to help?' I asked. The major said that he would like us to stand down from our present task of perimeter defence and get ready for a probable Jap landing. He explained that the local ack-ack batteries would have to deal with a Jap air attack on China Bay but the coast was virtually unguarded. He added that my sector was about 136 miles long. He hadn't, at that moment, the foggiest idea where the Nips would land but, when they did, would I very kindly, with my 110 men, hurl them back into the sea. 'How will you go about this?' he enquired. 'By taking a long holiday,' I felt like telling him.

Obviously I couldn't possibly cover 136 miles of coastline with 110 men so I said I would first need a signal section to be attached to me so that I could keep in radio contact. Then I would move to the middle of my sector and await signals telling me where the landing or landings were expected and I would arrange as hostile a reception as I could.

When the major had left me, and I was alone, I realized I was quite shaken and I realized that I had possibly a week to live at the most. This was bad enough, but how on earth could I tell my young soldiers of the early and sticky end that awaited them? I mustered the whole company in a mess-hall and gave them what must have been the most corny patriotic speech I could concoct in the short time I had. It went down well and I was very proud of 'D' Company.

My quartermaster broke out the rum and we set to work to move out to our sector. Weapons were cleaned and oiled, ammunition distributed, rations loaded onto trucks and the other 101 arrangements made to move into action.

On arrival at our sector's middle I gave Intelligence our map reference and we waited – and waited – and waited. Nothing happened and Intelligence told me that the Japs had altered course and were no longer heading for us. It was assumed that as their cover had been blown by the Catalina, the Japs had to think again. In the event they raided Colombo Harbour a few days later – on Easter Sunday morning to be precise – and did quite a lot of damage, sinking a destroyer at her moorings and some merchant vessels as well. On Easter Monday I was ordered to move 'D' Company to Colombo to guard Ratmalana Aerodrome and whilst we were on the way down, the Japs raided China Bay Aerodrome. I seemed to be leading a charmed life and missing all the action.

We heard afterwards that the Japs were very surprised by the extent of the opposition their invasion fleet encountered and they had no idea we had Spitfires, Hurricanes, Beauforts and some American bombers and fighters as well. They believed their whole intelligence about the strength of India and Ceylon was hopelessly wrong and so they turned tail and sailed back to Singapore I imagine.

Whilst on the subject of the attack on Colombo Harbour by the Japs, I was sitting next to a man at a masonic dinner one evening after the war had ended. He told me that he was a diver employed by the Colombo Port Commission and I asked him if he had had many scary adventures during his diving work – you know, like over-sexed octupuses grabbing him by the neck, etc. He said one of the worst experiences he had ever had was whilst he was examining the destroyer sunk by the Japs – in the harbour on Easter Sunday morning. He explained that the destroyer had been sunk whilst still at her moorings in very shallow water; so shallow that the destroyer's bridge, funnel, masts, etc were still above water and she was resting on the bottom. It follows – my friend went on – that he could see very clearly under water with the sun streaming down on the surface. He got to the ward-room door and to open it he had to push very hard on account of the weight of water in the room. In doing so he started a wave, or eddy, in the room and he said he nearly died of shock, when four naval officers, still in their white shirts and shorts rose from the ward-room breakfast table and came to the door to meet him. They had been killed by concussion the previous morning and so they were still perfectly preserved by the sea water and my friend said it was a terrible shock.

Once 'D' Company had arrived in Colombo we were transported to Ratmalana, a distance of only ten miles or so south on the west coast. Here I learned that General Henry Pownall was dissatisfied with the perimeter protection of the aerodrome and wanted the defences tightened up considerably. I was proud that 'D' Company had been selected and the company commander I was replacing took it all very well – far better than I would have done. I met General Pownall a day or so later and he told me exactly what he wanted done and I then gave him lunch and he departed. I was not feeling too well on that morning and after lunch I put my second-in-command in charge and told him I was going to have a rest. The next thing I knew was a doctor standing by my bed and my batman packing a suitcase for me. I was taken to hospital – an old convent – and a very saucy young blonde nurse said, 'And what can I do for you?' 'I'm not feeling too good, nurse,' I said. 'Oh, you poor boy,' she said – sarcasm dripping from every word – 'You see these wounded airmen? Now *they* are *really* not feeling too good and we're very short of space – are you sure you can't carry on without being admitted?' 'I don't know what's wrong,' I said, 'but our battalion doctor has sent me here so why don't you take it up with him?' She took me to one of a number of empty beds, made me sit down, and shoved a thermometer in my face. She took it out, read it, and went bright red. I was 104 degrees. I had malaria, from China Bay, and her attitude changed abruptly and she became quite human.

Two things happened to me in that hospital – one funny and one not funny. The first one was on one morning, about a week later when I was allowed my first solid food. This was breakfast and it consisted of two small slices of fried bread and on each was a rolled up piece of fried bacon. Normally, I would have scoffed them both without looking but not this morning – I was starving and they had to last. So I daintily unrolled one piece of bacon – inside was a large and well-fried cockroach – its brother was in the other roll. I decided I'd wait for lunch.

The other thing happened just as I was about to be discharged – the head MO came up and said there had been an unfortunate incident and as a captain was involved I would have to stay and guard him because I was the only other officer in the hospital of equal rank. It appeared that the captain in charge of the Colombo area NAAFI (a sort of army Tesco if you like) had been cooking the books for months and selling stuff on the black market. This character had heard the evening before that an audit team was about to visit him to check up on his books and stock and this was not to his liking at all. So he cut his throat. The matron was particularly incensed – 'Why on earth can't people cut their throats properly?' she muttered. 'They always put their heads back to do it – this tightens all the muscles of the throat and you can never do a thorough job – if only they'd put their heads down, throat-cutting is easy.' I expect she knew best but I didn't admire her attitude.

Anyway, the man was violent and after they had stitched him up they had to bandage his hands because he kept on trying to open up his neck again. So I had to sit by his bed and watch him like a hawk. I was feeling very groggy myself after my malaria and I didn't enjoy guarding the suicide merchant. I wasn't relieved until late that night and my relief was someone I knew well, in fact one of the eight CPRC people who became CLI captains. He arrived with a book and I explained he'd have no time for reading because our friend was a very cunning and determined character. However, my relief thought he knew best and whilst he was reading in the middle of the night the NAAFI wallah slipped out of bed, he was on the first floor, rushed to the verandah and threw himself over. He still didn't die at once but after a day or two he developed pneumonia and succumbed.

Back I went to 'D' Company at Ratmalana aerodrome which was all very boring because nothing of any importance happened and I still felt I could be of more use in Burma. The other seven captains were all bored as well for the same reason and we all seemed to do nothing but guard duties. At least I was lucky because I got on very well with my battalion commander and his staff and, of course, my own company. This was not the case with some of the others who seemed to find it difficult to settle down in their battalions.

There was a Spitfire Squadron, No. 273, amongst all the other squadrons at Ratmalana and their adjutant, a man called Bob Wasey, was an old planter friend of mine. As a result I was a frequent visitor at the 273 Mess and I even played hockey for them on occasions against the other squadrons. I used to have my leg pulled unmercifully. For instance, one evening they were talking about the difficulties of flying through thick cloud because if one's instruments were on the blink one didn't know if one was upside down or not. I found this hard to believe and said so – I said surely if one was upside down one's harness would dig into one's shoulders etc, etc. I added they were all potty and shouldn't they be looking for other jobs? At this stage the squadron commander, a South African charmer called Connie Constantine, intervened and said, 'It's quite true, Alan, why only yesterday I was doing about 300 knots in my Spit in thick cloud, when a flock of geese overtook me with their legs in the air!' I gave up.

About this time the word 'prang' became fashionable in RAF chat in the mess. I had no idea what it meant and so, one evening, in my innocence, I enquired. I should have known better. 'It's a sort of short Malayan dagger,' said someone. 'No, it's not,' said someone else, 'it's a fruit found in the Desert of Sind.' 'What absolute rubbish,' said a third. 'It's a small wild cat found in the Burmese jungles.' Once again, I gave up. A month or so later I was doing my rounds of the aerodrome and checking that my little soldiers were on their toes when I saw a Hurricane coming in to land with only one wheel down. The other had jammed in the retracted position. I dashed to the far end of the runway to see if I could help the pilot when the Hurricane finally came to rest. In fact the plane shot off the runway, having dug in a wing, and ended up in a paddy-field at about 100 knots and in small pieces. The pilot, quite unharmed, got out and struggled through the thick paddy-field mud to the runway. By this time an ambulance, a fire engine and crowds of people had arrived. I was watching when a hand fell on my shoulder. It was Connie Constantine. 'Alan,' he said, pointing to the wreckage, ' *That's* a prang.'

One evening I was invited to a party in a Beaufort squadron mess. The CO asked me whether I would like to fly with him in the second pilot's seat, or navigator's seat, during an exercise the squadron was taking part in a few days' time. I jumped at it and presented myself at the crack of dawn at the mess on the appointed morning. I should explain that a Beaufort is a light twin-engined torpedo bomber capable of doing 250 plus knots. The exercise was an assumption that a Japanese fleet of warships had been spotted 100 or so miles off the west coast of Ceylon and that the squadron was to intercept it, attack it and do as much damage as they could. The CO led me to his plane, installed me in the co-pilot's seat next to him and off we went, about 12 Beauforts in all.

We flew at about 250 knots, only ten or twelve feet above the sea to avoid the 'enemy' fleet's radar. This was hair-raising enough but the CO kept on using his cheesecutter to trim the aeroplane. A cheesecutter is a wheel above the pilot's head and one turns it to adjust the trim of the plane. It was terrifying because instead of the wretched man looking to see where he was going he was looking upwards at his dreaded cheesecutter. We were going so fast – umpteen feet a second is a speed that embarrasses sight – that I could not focus on the waves streaming under our nose and then, of course, there were more Beauforts on either wing tip only a few feet away. Actually it was exhilarating beyond belief.

I first saw the 'enemy' when they were about ten miles away and as we were travelling at about four miles a minute it was not long before we reached them. Although the fleet was supposed to be Japanese it consisted of two RN cruisers and four destroyers. My pilot, the CO, had already issued his attack plan and we dropped back and watched other Beauforts go in first to drop their torpedoes and then take immediate and violent evasive action. Our turn came and in we went at what seemed to me like nought feet, fired our torpedo and climbed steeply over a cruiser. It was all over in a few minutes and we got into formation again and set off for home. What I did not expect was that some twenty or thirty miles from base we were attacked by 'enemy' fighters, in fact Spitfires and Hurricanes. I had never been in a dogfight before and we seemed to be attacked by a number of fighters simultaneously. I could see other Beauforts being attacked and my pilot was yelling out warnings to his squadron on the inter-com – he seemed to love every second of the engagement and threw our aeroplane about all over the sky with great abandon. I wasn't actually ill but I felt very very sick indeed and needed a restorative or three when we got home.

One or two things had happened by this time – late 1942. I had sold my insurance agency to old man Kitching and the MG had been swapped and I had a Riley Kestrel Saloon at Ratmalana. This latter was in great demand by some of the 273 squadron people, Peter Kershaw, Bob Wasey and others, to take their popsies out on dates. I shudder to think of some of the goings-on in that poor car – however there *was* a war on and one had to be generous.

I was getting more and more bored with aerodrome defences and longed for some action and it was about this time that 273 squadron got their orders to go to Burma – to the Arakan to be precise. I went and saw Connie Constantine at once and asked him to take me to Burma with the squadron in any capacity. He said he would with pleasure but it would mean resigning my commission and becoming an aircraftsman in the RAF, ie the equivalent of a private soldier. I said 'done' and wrote to Col Martenstyn explaining how frustrated I felt, how much I wanted to fight and would he please agree to release me. He was very nice about it and said he was on the verge of making me his adjutant but if I was determined he would put my case before the regimental commander. The next thing that happened was that I was summoned to Base Area in Colombo and duly appeared before Col Griffith the RCO. 'What's all this nonsense?' he asked. I started to explain but he cut me short by saying Brigadier Gough, the Base Area Commander, wanted to see me. 'What on earth for, sir?' I asked. 'I'm only a miserable captain and my second-in-command is quite capable of taking over "D" Company at Ratmalana.' No good – and off we went to see Brigadier Gough – a small, practically square man with a glass eye and an M.C. and some First World War medals on his chest, just below his parachute wings. He looked me up and down, smiled and said, 'Sit down, Bayne.' I did and he opened my file which he already had in front of him before I was taken in. 'I hear you want to leave the army, Bayne, and join the ranks in the RAF.' I said I did and explained why for the umpteenth time. 'You've got a good record and Colonel Griffith speaks well of you – he also says you know your jungles and have spent many holidays in them before the war,' said the Brigadier. I simpered suitably. 'Well – now listen to me, Captain Bayne,' Brigadier Gough said, and he went on, 'General Wingate, as you know, has done marvellous work in Burma with his Chindits, and his long-range penetration patrols have gone well behind the Japanese lines and have done a lot of damage to their lines of communication in general and to their morale in particular. General Wingate has a jungle school in India where the instructors are ex-Chindit column leaders and I want a similar school in Ceylon. Colonel Griffith had already given me your name before your request for transfer came in and he feels you would be the right man to start my jungle school. I would want you to commandeer a suitable stretch of land, choose your officers and staff, read up all you can about Wingate's ideas on jungle warfare and get things moving at once. You will be Commandant and I will ask HQ in Delhi to promote you to lieutenant-colonel. I will instruct my GII and GIII here to give you anything you want – Do you still want to join the RAF?' '*No sir,*' I said.

I could not believe my good luck and I took the view that if my eye stopped *me* from mixing it with the Japs at least I could teach other people how to do it. I suggested to Brigadier Gough that I should be released from 'D' Company at once and given a day or two to hand over to the new company commander. I said I would like to report back to him within a week to lay my ideas and plans before him so that I would be sure of starting off on the right foot. This was agreed and the following week I had my ideas cut and dried and laid a broad plan of what I was going to do before Brigadier Gough and this too was agreed and approved by him. In my plan I made two important points to be implemented as soon as possible – first that I should be sent to Wingate's Jungle School in India as a student and, secondly, I should be seconded or attached to a regiment in action in Burma against the Japs for some weeks as soon as the school was running. Cunning old Bayne – Burma at last.

Before going any further, it is well worth while, I think, to set out a few facts about the remarkable Gough family: Brigadier Gough, 'Bill' to his friends, had, and still has, a niece called Denise and here's where the remarkable facts come to light. Denise's father was General Sir Hubert Gough, his brother, (and Denise's uncle) was General Sir John Gough V.C., her grandfather was General Sir Charles Gough V.C. and her great-uncle was General Sir Hugh Gough V.C. Three V.C.s in a family must surely be a record. Denise, who lives only five minutes away, and is our very good friend, once told me that she and her sister were at Sandhurst, attending a ceremony for holders, past and present, of the Victoria Cross. An Australian couple, whom we also know very well, sat down at Denise's table, and the lady enquired what Denise and her sister were doing at a V.C. ceremony and she explained *she* was there to represent her husband who holds a V.C. Denise said quietly, 'As a matter of fact my sister and I are here to represent our family who hold three V.C.s!'

To return to the embryo jungle school – first I decided on what staff I would need – they would have to be young, very fit and durable – and I knew that some of the eight CPRC people who, with me, took commissions in the CLI were unhappy where they were and, as a nucleus I selected three to fill the roles of chief instructor, adjutant and senior instructor. I also selected three regular warrant officers, the senior being RSM Grindley of the Royal Welsh Fusiliers. The GII at Base Area put an office at my disposal and gave me a secretary and I set to work. I was also given transport and a driver and I called on my proposed officers and WOs to put them in the picture and to invite them to leave their present duties and join me. They all leapt at it. I then started looking for a suitable location and found exactly what I needed about twenty miles from Colombo. It was a plantation of about 300 or 400 acres and it was planted up with coconut trees, rubber trees and cashew nut trees.

The most important feature of the property, so far as I was concerned, was the fact that it was very hilly and rocky. This meant that I could exercise three platoons, all using ball ammunition, grenades and two inch mortars, at the same time without any one platoon shooting up another platoon. It sounds hairy but in fact in two and a half years I had no casualties and this was pretty good considering I used over 100,000 rounds of .303 ammunition alone each three week term. The name of the property was Danaw Kande and, apart from a number of small buildings, there was a very large house occupied by the owners. From the condition of the property it was obvious it was not a paying proposition and the proprietors seemed delighted at the news that I was going to commandeer it for the duration of the war and that they would be paid compensation for any damage we did when the war was over.

Base Area was most efficient and soon the place was swarming with engineers, contractors, builders, etc. They built *cadjan* huts for living accommodation for my staff and students – nearly 300 of us in 'term' time. The huts were about 100 feet long with concrete floors and with a wooden framework clad with cadjans on the roofs and walls. A *cadjan* is a whole coconut tree leaf with the fronds plaited to make a quite waterproof thatched 'sheet'. My officers' quarters were the same, only better, if you follow me and my own quarters, as is only right and proper, were better still. I brought out my bed, cocktail cabinet, radiogram, rugs, etc from my parents' house in Colombo and I was very comfortable. I once heard my adjutant referring to it as 'Jeanette Macdonald's boudoir'. Sour grapes! In about two months we were ready and during this time Base Area was busy arranging for our first intake of students. There were 110 of them from various British regiments and the Royal Marines and Royal Air Force. We were sent officers, warrant officers and sergeants only. Apart from our 'jungle drill' and 'battle drill' areas we had a very strenuous assault course and a terrifying obstacle course. We used explosives (gun-cotton) and live ammunition to smarten up the students on the assault course but the obstacle course needed no such refinements.

In addition to my officers and staff I had a platoon of CLI troops (thirty-two men) as my 'enemy' platoon. They dressed in Jap uniforms and, when in contact with the students, they invented their own language which they fondly imagined sounded like Japanese. They were very effective and provided me with a most useful 'enemy' and they were commanded by a most efficient sergeant called Loos.

We had a three week course every month and then a week off to 'make and mend' and get ready for the next intake. There was always a lot of work to be done in our week 'off'.

We had over 3,000 students through our hands whilst I was commandant and I hope we did some good. I believe we did because battalions were queueing up to send students every term and we became notorious to the extent that visiting brass hats, war correspondents and news cameramen became a perfect nuisance. They had to have a sort of 'nanny' attached to them to see they came to no harm. My staff and I were busy enough without such interruptions. Looking through my visitors' book I see we had the following 'top brass': colonels, RN captains and RAF Wing-commanders and below are too numerous to mention.

Commander-in chief	1	
Generals	1	
Lt Generals	1	
Major Generals	4	
Brigadiers	14	
RN Admirals	1	
Air Commodore RAF	1	
WRNS Officers	8	(*No* trouble or bother)

With regard to our Wren visitors, you remember the old saying 'Up with the lark and to bed with a Wren'? When we were on our week's break between courses, my adjutant used to send a signal to Wren HQ in Colombo saying there would be a curry lunch party in the officers' mess on a certain Sunday and we would be delighted to see any Wrens (Officers or otherwise) who were brave enough to attend. We sent a truck and usually got twelve or fifteen Wrens in our net.

Some of the officers in the new Spitfire squadrons at Ramalana (some of whom had already been to the school as students) usually got to hear of our lunch parties and a flight of three Spitfires would 'beat up' our mess and drop messages in empty Very light cartridges with streamers. Very rude messages too as a rule. It was all illegal and highly dangerous because they used to fly over at 300 knots at palm tree height to drop their messages. The Wrens loved it.

After two weeks at the school listening to lectures, watching demonstrations, getting fit and learning about the jungle and the Japs, the whole school would move to the real jungle about a hundred miles away. Here a student would be selected to be company commander and I would decide who would be his platoon commanders, NCOs, etc. He would be given a task of raiding a village eight or ten miles away, destroying it, taking prisoners and retiring to Base without being caught. My 'enemy' platoon dressed in their Jap suits, would intercept, harass and generally torment the students on the way to the task and on the way back. The students had to signal for two airdrops of rations, one on the way to the task and once on the way back. This was a godsend for the 'enemy' – they would see the aeroplane arriving, watch the little parachutes come down and then move in and give the students hell just as they were distributing their rations.

I don't propose to bore you with my two and a half years at the school but one or two incidents may amuse you.

Actually the first incident is not funny at all, simply unfortunate. One day my RSM came down to my quarters and asked if he could speak to me in confidence. I sat him down, gave him a beer and asked him what the trouble was. It seemed my adjutant was making a nuisance of himself, late at night, by visiting the WOs and sergeants' messes, drinking their NAAFI rations, spreading untruthful rumours and generally making a nuisance of himself. The next day I confronted the officer concerned – he broke down and admitted all. He was back on his way to his battalion within the hour. It was such a pity but it was the demon drink at the bottom of it. He had been to one of our three top public schools.

My RSM Jack Grindley, made me laugh one day. He was in the orderly room with my adjutant and me and we were discussing promotions in my 'enemy' platoon. 'How about Private Fernando, Mr Grindley?' I asked. 'He's ready for a stripe I think.' 'Oo Sir? – you mean Private Fernando of No. 2 section?' 'Yes,' I said. Said Mr Grindley, 'Sir, if that private's brains was dynamite, they wouldn't blow his cap orf!'

Then, one evening we were just about to go to bed when the phone in my quarters rang. It was the duty officer and he had had a phone call from the local police station to say that two very suspicious characters had walked into a Buddhist temple a few miles away and were asleep there. They were armed to the teeth. We knew at the time that German officers were in Japan helping to train the Nips and my duty officer had said one man was a Jap and the other a large red-faced white man. As quietly as I could I told my DO to arrange with the guard commander to have a small truck, seven men, armed with rifles, ready in ten minutes and I was on my way to the guard room. My second-in-command, Lawrence Harvey, and my new adjutant, Roy Webber, were at my door – they had heard every word. 'Can we come too, Sir?' they pleaded. Well, they wanted some action as badly as I did so I said, OK. We arrived at the temple, guarded the doors, and tip-toed in. Sure enough – our two lovelies were fast asleep on the floor with sten guns beside them. Both were in khaki shirts and slacks but had no badges of rank. One was large, red and bucolic looking and could easily have been a Nazi – the other was slitty-eyed, yellowish and looked very Nipponese. I gave the large one a nudge with my boot and he awoke. I advised him to take things very easily and hand me his identity card. He said in good English that he hadn't got one and who was I anyway? His oriental mate had come to by this time and he had no identity card either. On questioning the large one he said he was a member of Force 136 (a splendid cloak and dagger outfit) and that he and his friend were testing out a new ration pack to see for how long it supported a well-laden soldier on the march. I thought this to be a load of balony and told him so – I added they were both under arrest and would they kindly accompany me. The modest show of truculence they then put up was short-lived and they sensed, I think, my little escort was getting restless and perhaps a trifle trigger-happy. I took them under guard for the night. I phoned the duty officer at Base Area in Colombo and told him the story. He was very excited and I said I'd have both men at Base Area early in the morning. When we arrived – prisoners, escort, the lot – there was quite a crowd waiting and we were ushered into Brigadier Gough's room. There was a Colonel Williams (I think) present and to my great sorrow he recognized both men at once and confirmed they were in fact his people. Brigadier Gough then stepped in and tore them off a strip and told them they were stupid to travel without identification of any sort and that they were extremely wise not to have given any resistance to arrest. A very tame ending and a disappointing one. However, I got a pat on the back.

During the war I was sent to a small arms school in central India at a place called Saugur. At the end of the course there was a three or four day long patrol and they said to me that I could skip the patrol if I was ready to man a crossing-point alone for three nights somewhere in the middle of India. I agreed and set up my little bivouac under a large tree which was literally in the middle of nowhere. About the second day patrols started passing through my point and I would mark their cards with the appropriate times on them. One evening I was all alone when a Hindu gentleman appeared out of the blue. I was having my supper of bully beef and biscuits when he came up to me, squatted down on his hunkers and started chatting. My Hindustani wasn't too hot but somehow we made ourselves understood and he asked me what I was eating. I said meat and biscuits and he asked whether he could have some. Naturally I agreed and he enjoyed a pretty hearty meal. At the end he thanked me very much and asked me what was it exactly he had been eating. I showed him the bully beef tin which had a picture of a large horned bull on the front. My Hindu guest spat violently, picked up his dhoti and hared over the horizon at great speed.

One morning Brigadier Gough arrived and took me aside. 'Captain Bayne,' he said, 'I have some disappointing news for you – Delhi won't agree to your being a lieutenant-colonel but they've agreed to you being a Major and I have back-dated your appointment by eight months.' I was disappointed, of course, but the eight months' back-pay was useful! One morning a signal came through to the effect that I had been given a place at General Wingate's school in Mysore, India. My joining instructions were more than clear on the matter of physical fitness with great emphasis being laid on the intake of salt to prevent exhaustion. The school was just outside the small town of Shimoga, inland from the west coast of India (Mysore State) and north of Mangalore where the famous tiles come from. As I think I've said, the commandant and instruc-

99

tors were all ex-Chindits and ex-leaders of the long-range penetration columns Wingate sent into Burma. The school was in thick jungle of the most inhospitable variety and it was the first time I had ever seen bamboo with one inch thorns sticking out. As in my school there were 110 students consisting of officers, VCOs, warrant-officers and sergeants and so we were in effect a company strong. We were all sorts and nationalities and, for instance, I shared a room with a Sikh captain. I used to watch fascinated whilst this character tied up his hair and whiskers at night – Sikhs are not allowed to cut any hair and he used to take ages over his toilette.

Shimoga too had an 'enemy' company and they also dressed up as Japs. They were Dogras from northern India and first-class fighting soldiers they were too. Their commanding officer was a Major Hastings, Irish Guards, and he was cold towards me at first but we parted good friends at the end of the three week course. I'll explain in a minute. The first afternoon we were given a short patrol to see what the Mysore jungle was like. We were divided up into sections (seven men in each) with an instructor. On water discipline, we were told to drink from our water bottles as much as we liked but when the bottle was empty that was it – there was no other water anywhere. I have never encountered heat and humidity like Mysore anywhere else in the world. My battledress was sopping wet after an hour or so with sweat and my water had gone too. By the time the exercise ended I was a little thirsty. A student – a major – not in my section – started behaving strangely after a few hours. He started attacking the prickly bamboo with his machete, then he started frothing at the mouth. His section and instructor made a make-shift stretcher, tied him down on this with rifle slings and carried him back to camp. He died a few hours later in an ambulance on his way to hospital in Bangalore. The post-mortem showed he had died of exhaustion because he was not fit and had not had his proper salt intake.

The course was very very tough but although I was one of the more senior officers, one of only three majors, I was never given any command of any importance. I took this up with the commandant and he told me not to worry and that I was going to lead the final five day patrol at the end of the course. This turned out to be a company exercise, that is to say all 110 students and the platoon and section commanders were chosen by the school. The task was to destroy a strongly held 'Japanese' village some seventeen miles from the school with thick jungle and two rivers intervening. I was given details of the task on the afternoon of the day before the patrol started off. I called up my 'O' group of platoon and section commanders and my signals section and put them in the picture. I was nervous because at this stage I had never been in battle and the school commandant and all the instructors were present, all of whom had been in contact with the Japs in Burma.

The only instructor not present was Major Hastings the 'enemy' commander. I gave my orders and outlined the route we would take to the task, the probable way in which we would cross both rivers, the method I would use on the assault of the village and I said I would give orders for our return to base later on. We started off at the crack of dawn on D1 and cut our way through thick jungle and scrub for four miles using a compass to keep direction. On nearing a main road we had to cross I sent a party of four Ghurka VCOs forward as a reconnaissance patrol to find out how far the road was ahead and to tell me where and how far a certain milestone was. They were back in an hour and said the road was about a quarter of a mile ahead and my milestone was 200 yards to our right, not bad compass work through thick jungle. We then came to our first river which was fordable – more jungle and then our second river which was in flood. The water was chest-high and the current very strong – to make matters worse we were carrying full equipment, arms and ammunition and some people couldn't swim. I decided on a night crossing and sent a strong swimmer across carrying a thin line – once he was across we made all our rifle slings into a 'rope' and the swimmer on the far bank – say fifty yards away – towed the slings across and made them fast. We then had a 'chain' across the river. We all got over and were very wet and cold. We laid up for the rest of the night and set off at first light on D2 towards our target. We must have made good progress because I was not far away by evening. Once again I called up my faithful group of four Ghurkas and told them to look at the target and come back and report. They did and said the 'Japs' were having a high old time and making lots of noise and so it was clear to me that Major Hastings was not expecting me until D3.

I called up my 'O' group (all instructors present!) and said I was in a perfect position to carry out the task completely with few or no casualties and so I would move in at once. Here the chief instructor stopped me and explained that, whilst he could not fault my planning, if I did attack now I would completely ruin the exercise because we would be through the village like a dose of salts and there would be no opposition. I said, 'Too bad,' but this is how any commander would act with the enemy at his mercy. He agreed but insisted that I wait until first light. I sent for my 'O' group again and gave fresh orders for a dawn attack. I also arranged for an air-drop of rations through my signal section and laid out my plan for our withdrawal after the attack. I ordered a 'fade' by platoons, leaving it to the platoon commanders to decide for themselves if they wanted, in addition, their sections to fade separately. A 'fade' is where the attacking force, after the attack, breaks up and goes different ways to shake off the enemy and then re-groups at a pre-arranged RV (rendezvous) at a given time. Our RV was of course the spot fixed for our air-drop and I warned platoon commanders another fade might be necessary after that and we agreed on a second RV. Of course, the air-drop would be a dead giveaway for Major Hastings and his 'Japs' so I made it as hard as possible for him. All went well – our light plane arrived at the map-reference dead on time, dropped our rations and pushed off. We collected and distributed our goodies as fast as possible and faded. When we re-grouped, my platoon and section commanders reported they had seen neither hide nor hair of the enemy so I hoped Major Hastings enjoyed himself looking for us.

I realized I was now a whole day early in the exercise and that I could be back at base on D4 instead of D5 if we pushed on hard and crossed both rivers by bridge instead of fording them. Accordingly I went to the chief instructor, a Major Ross, and said if it was OK by him I'd like to push on hard for base. This, to my delight was agreed and we laid on an assault attack on both bridges, in case they were 'occupied', but, yet again, no Major Hastings! We reached base intact on the evening of D4 very pleased with ourselves for having foxed the enemy who knew that bit of Shimoga much better than we did.

At the closing address, when we were all back in our proper uniforms, the commandant was very complimentary and said we were the first student wing ever to have avoided the 'enemy' for the entire way home. Major Hastings said to me, 'Where the hell did you get to?' I showed him on my map and we parted good friends.

My 'report' from Shimoga went straight to Brigadier Gough – they had given me a 'Distinction' and said if I ever wanted to go back as an instructor they would be glad to have me. I purred.

A few weeks later I was told that I'd been posted, temporarily, to a battalion of the Frontier Force Rifles in Burma. At last! I left Lawrence Harvey in charge of the school and left for Calcutta on the first leg of my journey. From Calcutta I made my way in short hops by air to Chittagong, Cox's Bazaar, Akyab and Ramree. I met up with my battalion in Ramree and then in an assortment of landing craft we crossed to the Arakan coast and landed at Taungup. A strange thing happened at Cox's Bazaar – I was waiting on an airstrip to cadge a lift to Akyab when I saw a squadron of Spitfires deployed under camouflage netting. There was a mechanic working on one and I showed him my identity paper and asked him which squadron it was. '273 sir,' he said and I found it hard to believe the coincidence. 'Do you know a Flight Lieutenant Kershaw?' I asked. He pointed to a jeep coming towards us and said, 'If that's not Mr Kershaw with me bleedin' plugs, sir – there's going to be a row!' A small world because this was the Peter Kershaw from Ratmalana who so ill-used my poor Riley for his nefarious purposes.

I finally reached Ramree island and met up with my battalion. The CO and other officers made me very welcome and I was posted to a company commanded by a major whose name I forget. However, it would be impossible to forget him. He was of medium height, slim and his complexion was more red than brown, he had a hooked nose and the palest blue eyes I've ever seen. He might have been a Pathan from northern India but I remember thinking how glad I was to be on his side and not against him. His men adored him and he led from the front and I learnt a lot from his standards and qualities for the few weeks I fought with him.

We crossed to the Arakan coast in a Brigade assault and landed, with some opposition from the Japs, at a place called Taungup. Having dealt with the opposition, we started on the road to Rangoon clearing up the Japs as and when we met them. I felt a bit nervous at first and found it all a bit hairy but soon settled down and thoroughly enjoyed myself. We were a brigade group and we consisted of ourselves (Frontier Force Rifles), the Green Jackets, the Royal Artillery and a third battalion whose identity I forget.

I was given a Pathan batman who was a great little chap and a very fierce soldier. He never left my side and I was terribly sad when, one Sunday evening, during an attack on a hill held by the Nips, he had his head nearly taken off his shoulders by a burst of machine-gun fire. He died in my arms.

One day we were moving through a Burmese village which the Japs had vacated a few days earlier. Life was returning to normal and the village shops were starting to do business again. The shops were on stilts, because of flooding, and each shop had a flat platform, also on stilts, in front of it on which the wares were displayed. Also being displayed on the platforms were the shop ladies. These were the most attractive and immaculate Burmese women of varying ages but all quite beautiful. Their black hair was sleeked back and most had a flower behind her ear. They wore spotless white lace blouses – very tight – and shiny black skirts leaving a bare midriff. They sat cross-legged and I leave you to imagine the effect they had on our column. We were young, very fit and hard and we hadn't seen a female for ages. It was all too much and I was having the most un-social emotions. Suddenly I noticed that almost every lady had a large Burma cheroot stuck in her face.

My carnal desires evaporated on the spot.

After a few weeks I was recalled and found the school a little dull after Burma. On the way home I spent a night or two in a transit camp in Barrackpore waiting for a plane for Colombo. I telephoned a good friend of mine called Oscar Andreae who was stationed in Calcutta and he invited me to dinner at the Bengal Club. My uniform looked like nothing on earth having been in my kitbag for some weeks but a dhobi at Barrackpore did wonders to it in half an hour. I met Oscar at the club and had the best dinner I had had for ages. I mean, only two days previously I had been sitting on any handy rock or mound in the jungle eating 'K' rations (not to be recommended) and now I was being offered Melba toast on a silver salver by a bearer in white gloves. Quite a contrast.

I found that my visits to Shimoga and Burma had made a big difference and I was now far more confident and I could lecture with more authority. However, this happy state of affairs didn't last long – Bill Gough, my brigadier was a 2nd/2nd Ghurka (King Edward VII's Own) and he was desperately proud of his regiment, and rightly so! He was very keen that I should visit them at their depot in Dehra Dun in the Himalayan foothills. As this was your great-uncle Vivian's regiment, even the same 2nd battalion, I packed my bags once more and departed.

As I've just said, Dehra Dun is at the foothills of the Himalayas in northern India. It stands at an elevation of 7,000 or 8,000 feet I suppose and the climate is lovely by day and very cold at night. High-level tea is grown around Dehra Dun and the jungle comes right down to the boundaries of the tea estates. On one of the night exercises I was taken on I remember lying out in the tea, freezing to death, and hearing a tiger call not far away. I froze even more – this time from fear.

I have always had the highest opinion of the Ghurka and, of course, their record in the First and Second World Wars has been almost without equal and V.C.s have been awarded *ad nauseam*. At least I was able to watch them training for war and it was all very impressive. I thought I was fit, I was certainly young, but the Ghurka is a hill-man and he can climb a mountain as if it were a molehill. I can't, and very tired I used to be at the end of the day. The senior VCO of the battalion was known as the Subahdar Sahib and he and I became great friends. One evening he asked me over to the VCOs mess for a drink, to the surprise of the British Officers – 'He doesn't speak English and you can't speak Ghurkali so how on earth will you get on?' they asked. 'He speaks very good English to me,' I said. 'The old fox,' they exclaimed, 'he pretends he doesn't understand a word.'

Anyway, off I went and I remember it was the most beautiful frosty moonlit night. It was a quarter of a mile walk to the VCO's mess and they had all put on their best uniforms – not full dress kit but almost. The Subahdar Sahib greeted me and offered me plain rum in a tumbler – it seemed a pretty hostile start to the evening but they were all knocking them back and so it seemed a good idea to join in. After a bit an orderly came up with a silver tray full of *pakhoras* – a sort of fried fritter made of lentil flour and spiced with onion and green chillies. Quite delicious and I was about to help myself to one, 'Not that one Sahib,' said the Subahdar Sahib, 'that one is very hot, try this one.' I suspected I heard a giggle from some of the young VCOs and I took the offered *pakhora* and wisely broke it in two. It was stuffed with *whole red* chillies and I suppose I ruined their little joke! After an hour I left and the freezing air hit me like a hammer – I'd had far too many straight rums and I could barely stand – I got back to our mess and went straight to bed.

Our mess was the most civilized affair and, at table, each officer had an orderly standing behind his chair. At breakfast the morning paper was propped up on a stand in front of one's place and dinner was grand beyond belief. It was a marvellous regiment and it was an education to see the detailed and realistic training that was given to the young riflemen to turn them into a most splendid fighting force more than capable of keeping up the most envied traditions of the 2nd/2nd Ghurkas. I was proud to have had an uncle who served with them and was killed in action with them.

To the north of Dehra Dun and 2,000 or 3,000 feet higher

106

lies Mussourie about a two hour drive away. This was where my sister Phyllys was born and I took a day off to go and have a look. I went by bus and the road is so narrow that a line of traffic goes one way up the hill for an hour and then another comes down during the next hour. The bus stopped at the foot of the town and everyone walked on from there. There were some rickshaws pulled by two men and pushed from behind by one, whilst coolies carried the most enormous loads on their backs secured by a folded piece of material round their foreheads. It made me feel quite weak even watching them.

I walked to the Imperial (?) Hotel for lunch and I stood on a balcony having a drink before going into the dining-room. It was a beautifully sunny day and I suppose I was standing at 10,000 feet and, although it was a little hazy, the whole Himalayan range lay before me. The mountains must have been 100 miles or so away but they were magnificent and they had a most curious effect on me. I felt sad and insignificant and very very lonely and I think it must have been the majesty and colossal size and magnificence of the range with some peaks wearing their crowns of the eternal snows that made me feel so sad. I went in and had lunch and a restorative or two before catching the bus home.

My visit to the 2nd/2nd Ghurkas finally came to an end and a few days later I was back at the Jungle School and made a full report to Bill Gough. Before leaving this matter of the 2nd/2nds, a coincidence happened a few months ago. Moose and I were invited to lunch by the Gartrells and I found myself sitting opposite our present CGS General (now Field-marshal) Sir John Chapple. He asked me if I'd seen anything of the war and I said I had and I happened to mention Dehra Dun. The reaction was electric – he too was a 2nd/2nd Ghurka and was fascinated when I mentioned Vivian Collins. Field-marshal Chapple looked up his records and wrote to me saying they had some information on Vivian, where he served, when and where he was killed in France, etc, and could I give him some more information for the official record. I sent him details about Vivian's exploits in the Himalayas and Assam and he wrote back very gratefully. A small world forsooth.

Back to 1945 and, although I did not know it at the time I returned from Dehra Dun, my days at the Jungle School were numbered and I only had a few more weeks of soldiering. We had a splendid 'house-clearing' drill at the school which was most exciting and dangerous. In our cashew nut plantation there was a moderately substantial house, a four up four down affair and it was empty, of course, because I had requisitioned the whole property. We had found in Burma that, on taking a village, some fanatical Japs usually remained behind to lay booby-traps and act as snipers and it was usually a problem to dislodge them. I got one or two ideas from books, added some of my own, and came up with a most effective way of removing unwanted temporary residents. The 'drill' was carried out by sections, ie seven men, and each man was armed with an automatic weapon and a '36' grenade. They would approach the house and throw in their grenades and as the dust and debris were settling they would rush in, kill any enemy they saw and then let loose a burst of automatic fire at the ceiling above their heads – in the form of an 'X'. This would, more often than not, kill anyone upstairs. Without hanging about, the section would then dash upstairs and deal with anyone still alive. We had model Japs, (stuffed dummies) in the downstairs rooms but we kept a surprise for the students upstairs.

As they rushed the stairs, Mr Grindley (my RSM) and I would fire bursts of tracer from a Bren past their heads to discourage further aggression. Mr Grindley and I were lying in a heavily sandbagged enclosure with the floor particularly protected, because we could always feel the automatic bullets hitting the sandbags under us when the students were cutting their 'X's downstairs. Once in the middle of an attack, the grenades had just gone off, the automatic fire was in full blast, dust was everywhere, plaster was coming down on us, the shouting and the din were appalling and we were waiting for the stairs to be rushed. Grindley turned to me and said, 'You know, sir, they would never be'ave like this if they was in their own 'omes.' Poor Lawrence Harvey, my second-in-command, got hit once by a '36' grenade during a 'drill'. He lost so much blood he nearly died. Luckily, I always kept my doctor and ambulance a few hundred yards away and after a week or two in hospital he came back to us.

Next door to the school was a battalion of Dogras camped on a coconut estate. As I think I've said before, the Dogra is a fine fighting soldier from the north of India and I know the Dogras' qualities in battle because I've seen them in action. They had a fine pipe band and although it seems incongruous for an Indian to be playing the bagpipes, their music was stirring enough in camp and it must have been even more so before a battle. The CO used to invite my officers and me to watch Beating Retreat occasionally and this ceremony consisted of marching and counter-marching, with tremendous precision, to the accompaniment of the band. Although we were supposed to be tough Jungle School instructors, hearing 'Over the sea to Skye' and other Scottish airs on the pipes left scarcely a dry eye amongst us. The pipers were always on the scrounge at my Q stores for golden syrup which they used to pour into their bagpipe skins to keep them supple. A nasty habit I used to think.

About this time my sister, who had been engaged for some time to a splendid Royal Marine captain, got married. They were married in Christ Church, Colombo where my father was vicar's warden, and the reception was at the Galle Face Hotel. I was best man and Bill Thurston (the groom) and I were posing for the photographers with my sister and parents when she looked Bill and me up and down and said to her new husband, 'I'm going to get to work on that waist of yours – look at Alan's Sam Browne – small and neat – you look like a sack of potatoes!' Harsh words from a wife of some sixty minutes or so. However, Bill rose to the occasion – he said, 'Well, someone in the family has got to look dignified!' Good for him.

On the matter of uniforms, from time to time we had visitors from the UK who used to turn up in the most super Savile Row uniforms made of gaberdine. These used to put our sweat-stained khaki or Jungle Green drill battledresses to shame and we were very jealous. Behind their backs we used to call them the Gaberdine swine.

Talking of the Royal Marines and my sister – about a year after the Jungle School started, Lawrence Harvey and I were having a weekend break in Bandarawela and on the Saturday evening we were having a drink in the Banderawela Hotel. At the next table were two Royal Marine captains and their girl-friends and they were talking quite loudly. Suddenly I heard my sister's name mentioned and so I pricked up my ears. One of the captains, who had obviously been slapped down at some stage or other by my sister, started on a most destroying description of Phyllys's habits and morals. He alleged among other things, that she was the easiest 'lay' in Colombo, etc, etc. Harvey put his hand on my arm at once and said, 'Don't do it – we're all in uniform and there'll be the most ghastly scene.' He was right, of course, but the injustice of what I'd just overheard – (my sister was the most prudish thing although very pretty and attractive) was too much for me. I went over and asked which one had talked about Phyllys Bayne. One said he had and I said, 'She's my sister – come outside.' I added, 'Bring your things with you – you won't be coming back.' I walked outside and he arrived a moment or two later. I told him what I thought of him. I told him his opinions were entirely wrong and I told him I was going to half-kill him. Well – his reaction was quite disgusting – he grovelled and he pleaded with me not to hit him and it was sickening to see an RM officer behaving like that. I told him to get a taxi and go before I changed my mind. He said, 'But my friends...' – I said I would tell his friends that he would not be returning. He went.

At the end of 1944 we were sent a whole wing of Royal Marine Commandos for 'special' training and it was very hush-hush. They were the most magnificent body of aggressive, athletic fighting men and my instructors and I had the devil's own job keeping up with them. I clamped down on security (although we had no idea what they were going to do) and I promised death and destruction to anyone at the school who talked. At the end of the course we were all on our knees with exhaustion and a special train was sent from Colombo to take the 100 strong group to Trincomalee. I gave special leave to my staff to go and see them off at the station because we had really grown very fond of them. I heard some weeks later that they were being prepared for a very special raid on the coast of Burma and they were going over by submarine first and then by inflatables on to the coast. As they were being finally briefed in Trinco someone *did* talk, the Japs were waiting for them and they were destroyed almost to a man. We felt it was a personal tragedy.

I wish I could remember exactly what it was, but I can't, and I can only think it was a parade I had to take to read out a letter or a message from the SEAC commander, Admiral Lord Louis Mountbatten. Anyway, my RSM laid on a full parade – students and all and I sent my car to Colombo to bring my father out to watch his offspring do his stuff. All went well and we had a party in our mess afterwards. I sent my father home after dinner and my mother rang me the next morning to ask what I had done to him because he was not at all well. She phoned again in the late afternoon to say my father was going to hospital for an operation because he was in great pain. I left for Colombo at once and went straight to the hospital. When I got there my father was already being operated upon and so I phoned my mother and sister at home and told them not to wait dinner for me because I would stay and see my father once he had left the operating theatre. In due course I saw him being wheeled down a corridor on his way back to his room. He looked very peaceful and I spoke to a Sinhalese nurse who was accompanying the trolley. 'How is my father?' I asked. She replied, 'He is dead.' The shock of that uncaring, callous little sentence was appalling. That was bad enough – I then had to go home and break the awful news to my mother and sister. It was simply dreadful.

I rang my second-in-command and asked him to carry on at the school and to tell Base Area I would be away for a day or so arranging my father's funeral. This took place the next evening and, quite unknown to me, my officers had arranged a full military funeral (my father had an M.B.E. for military work) with a firing party, a Union Jack for the coffin and a trumpeter. I had persuaded my mother and sister not to come

111

as it would be too much for my mother. I managed to control myself to nearly the end but after the volley over the grave the trumpeter sounded 'The Last Post'. This was too much for me and after one last salute I hurried away.

Vivian Collins in 1910 (second from left) before the Teram Kangri expedition.

The start of the Bombay to Poona trials in 1908. My father is in car No. 11.

The author's father in Pondicherry South India, 1906.

East Coast Jungle, in Ceylon 1935, with my tracker.

The author's mother
in her twenties.

The author's father,
in Bombay.

Colombo-Madras crews – 1937. The Colombo crew is on the right.

The Cox, 'Comrade' Sutherland, not long after this photo was taken was killed by a snake.

The MG18/80 in Colombo, 1937.

South West Monsoon Regatta, 1938. The author stroking the winning
crew.

The author driving the Riley *Imp* in the Mahagastotte Hill Climb, 1938

A home-made special in the Mahagastotte Hill Climb.

The author driving an MG in the Bogala Hill Climb, 1940.

Racing at Ratmalana Aerodrome in 1948. Author in No. 29.

A reprimand from a Marshal for not wearing a crash helmet.

The author's servants at *Shalimar* 1950. Left to right: Velu, Appu and Daniel.

Mike Henderson in the Lea-Francis, in a Round the Island Trial. It is 2am. Author navigating, 1950.

His Royal Highness the Duke of Edinburgh meeting the Committee of the Ceylon Chamber of Commerce, 1954.

With the $2\frac{1}{2}$ litre Riley in Colombo, 1954.

The Colombo Rowing Club Regatta arranged for Sir Eugene Millington-Drake, *Our Man in Monte Video*, Centre in 1955.

Moose when engaged to the author in 1958.

The family at Fairclose, 1968.

8

1945 – 1955
Hard Work and Play; Return to Civilian Life

The war against the Germans was about at an end and the Japanese were facing defeat too, although the events of Hiroshima and the atom bomb had still not taken place. So it was at about this time I paid a visit to my late father's firm to start looking into his affairs. The situation, as I found it, was depressing to say the least. I discovered that my dear old father had not changed his profligate ways at all since we had been in Sri Lanka, a matter of fifteen years. He and my mother had lived very well indeed with little or no thought to possible 'rainy days'. There was no life assurance (perhaps he was uninsurable because of his earlier cerebral malaria in Rangoon) and not a lot in the way of investments.

The situation was gloomy because I now had a widowed mother to look after and, having sold my insurance agency, I only had an Indian Army major's pay on which to do this. However, Providence was watching over me because, one morning – still in uniform, I was sitting at my father's desk sorting out old letters and things when the senior partner of the firm came over and sat down. He was one Dickie Richards and a man of considerable foresight and he had obviously appreciated the position I was in. 'Alan, what are you going to do now?' he asked. 'Get out of the army and find a job as soon as I can,' I replied. He said his partners and he had been thinking things over and wondered if I would like to take over where my father had left off. I couldn't believe my ears – or my good fortune. 'On what sort of terms, sir?' I asked. 'Oh, the same as your father of course – you'll be doing the same work and have the same responsibilities so it's only fair you should have the same terms – think about it.' 'I don't need to think about it, I'm most relieved and grateful and I accept with the greatest pleasure,' I said. Dickie Richards explained that I would be running the firm's insurance department and he hoped that, in due course, I would be made a 'per pro' and then a partner.

The firm was Leechman & Company and they were agents for a number of tea and rubber companies. They were, in effect, the link between the planter on his estate and the directors of the tea or rubber company in London. Leechmans had, in addition, an insurance department and a tea department and they were also agents for The Nuwara Eliya Brewery and a number of insurance companies. Our offices were in the Colombo business centre known as The Fort and we occupied the top floor of a large insurance building and we had a 300 degree view. This included the harbour and a large slice of the Indian Ocean and this could be a very pleasant distraction from one's work.

Having been offered a job I went at once to see my brigadier, poured out my woes and asked him to do what he could to have me demobilized on compassionate grounds because both wars were almost over. He was very good and I was a civilian again in two or three months. Before I left the brigadier I managed to have Lawrence Harvey and Roy Webber promoted to majors. The brigadier was no longer my splendid Bill Gough who, alas, was killed in a passenger plane somewhere over South Africa I think.

One last incident about Bill Gough before I leave the poor man alone. A few years ago Moose and I were lunching with an uncle of mine at Odiham. During lunch he asked me what I did during the war years and I gave him a thumb-nail sketch about the Jungle School. When I got to Bill Gough he seemed to be surprised and asked if he was a Ghurka. After lunch he disappeared for a minute or two while we were having coffee and re-appeared with a lady on his arm. 'This is my next-door neighbour, Alan,' he said. 'Bill Gough's widow.'

In the interval between being demobilized and joining Leechman's I looked for and found a small but attractive bungalow at a much lower rent than my parents' house. My sister joined her husband in Singapore and I moved my mother into our new house. I moved in too and I found it difficult to adjust to my new surroundings and the completely new way of life. Only a few weeks earlier and before my mother and I moved into Shalimar, I was looking after, and responsible for, a great number of men and things were done my way with no argument. Now I was alone with one elderly lady who had a will of her own and yet was timid and nervous about many things. Life was very very different.

We had three resident servants – first there was Appu, our head boy and cook, who had already been with my parents for some years, then there was a second servant and a house cooly. The dhobi called once a week and the garden was very small so we didn't have a resident gardener. Someone looked after it but it wasn't me. Under the eagle eye of Appu, the servants were remarkably honest and I never locked up anything and nothing was ever stolen. I used to give Appu money every morning at breakfast for the day's shopping and he would account in detail the next morning as to how he had spent it. We had a gentleman's agreement – he added on something to each item and I never queried it – I knew what was going on, so did he and he knew that I knew and that was that.

My work at Leechman's was not too strange because, having had my own insurance agency before the war, I was once again involved with insurance. However, I had not handled life assurance or marine insurance before and it took a little time getting used to these new classes.

I discovered that my father did a certain amount of assessing work and marine survey work and Leechman's were very generous in this. By this I mean I could take on as much of this 'extra-curricular' work as I wished provided it did not interfere with my Leechman's work. As I kept all the fees I earned I did nearly all my surveying and assessing work in the evenings. A lot of the marine survey work took me to the harbour warehouses and to the Indian bazaar shops in a street known as the Pettah. I would be appointed by an insurance company to look into a claim on which they had their doubts. I would make my investigations, sometimes in a hostile atmosphere, and send my report to the insurance company and, on the basis of this, they would either settle or repudiate the claim. I had many adventures as one can imagine and, to mention only one or two, the cunning of the consignees had to be experienced to be believed. On one occasion I was called to the Pettah, to an Indian silk shop, because the consignee (i.e. the man who had imported the goods) said he had had a consignment of fine English poplin delivered to his shop the previous day from the harbour and he suspected pilferage. There were three large packing cases and as the steel bands on two were missing and one was rather light in weight, the man said he thought they had been tampered with. I asked him had he opened any of the cases before I arrived and he said no, he hadn't, and thought it best to wait for me before doing so. Very right and proper! I had one case opened, the light one, and found chaos inside. There were only a few bolts of poplin inside and a large number of newspapers filling up the empty space. The newspapers were largely Indian – strange, because the consignment had come from England (although there was a large amount of Indian labour in the harbour warehouses) but I felt there was something fishy here. So I sat down and started going through all the papers, to the annoyance of the consignee who said it was getting late. I found, near the bottom, two things, first a copy of that morning's *Ceylon Daily News* and, secondly, a sheet of the consignee's own note-paper. I asked him how, if the cases had arrived the previous day and had not been opened before my arrival, *today's* paper could have got inside. Obviously, he had set up the whole affair himself. I said I was going straight to the police and he would be prosecuted for fraud. I left, and did another survey, and on reaching my car to go home there, on the back seat, were two lovely bolts of pale blue superfine poplin. I marched back to the shop, slammed the poplin on the counter and said I would now add bribery to the police charges. It was super poplin and I badly needed some new shirts. I *suppose* it pays to be honest.

116

During the time I was at Leechman's, nearly twenty years, I came across an awful lot of fraud, pilferage and dishonesty, and rackets there were in plenty. In about 1950 I became Chairman of the Colombo Marine Agents Association and at our AGMs I used to carry on like mad about the pilferage in the harbour and I used to tell the members that unless the Ceylon Government increased security arrangements in the port, marine insurance premiums to Colombo were going to go sky-high. My speech appeared in the papers every year but nobody ever did anything to improve conditions.

I was involved in one investigation once which I found fascinating – so much so that after it was all over I wrote a play about it. I took this to Radio Ceylon who bought the copyright and they then asked me to cast it for broadcasting. I did this, rehearsed it and Radio Ceylon recorded it and I was thrilled to hear it, more than once, over the air. The fees were good because I got the copyright fees, a fee for directing the play and another fee for acting in it.

To return to the investigation – this was the way of it. At about 9 am one day a friend of mine, another insurance wallah, came into the office and sat down at my desk. He was in a great state and asked me to help him because, he explained, as things stood at the moment there was a very good chance that he would be on the next boat to England. Sacked. He told me that a week earlier a gem merchant from Moratuwa came to his bungalow on the Saturday afternoon. He knew the gem merchant well and had previously insured many parcels of precious stones for him consigned to places all over the world. The gem merchant said that the previous afternoon he had sent a very valuable parcel of blue sapphires and star sapphires to Hatton Garden in London and had quite forgotten to arrange insurance. Pat Frisby, my shaken friend, told me that as he knew the man so well he had no hesitation in giving him cover at once and he posted a cover-note to the gem dealer on the Monday morning. The sum insured was immense, something over two million rupees and, although I might be quite wrong here (it was a long time ago) I seem to recollect that there was something like 800 carats of blue sapphires and over 1,000

117

carats of star sapphires in the parcel. Frisby put a cable on my desk which was from the consignees in Hatton Garden and it said, bleakly, that a parcel had arrived containing seven steel nuts and bolts and what was going on? Frisby said, 'You've simply got to get me out of this, Alan, or else I've had it.' I told him at once there seemed to be little I could do – I explained that the parcel was not available for inspection, I didn't know anything about the gem merchant so what *could* I do? – it was all too late. I said I would think about it and that I would phone him later on that morning. This I did and asked him to cable London at once and ask the consignees to send me the parcel, box, brown paper, string, sealing wax, nuts and bolts and all. It turned up in a few days' time by airmail. The parcel consisted of a cigar box with a neat hole cut in the bottom, it was lined with cotton wool and the steel nuts and bolts were, in fact, just steel nuts and bolts. The brown paper had a hole in it which corresponded to the hole in the box and this was hidden by the green customs declaration label.

Next I arranged an appointment with the gem dealer in Moratuwa, a place some fifteen or twenty miles south of Colombo. He seemed a nice old boy, a Muslim, and he made me welcome. I explained I was acting for the insurance company who had insured his gems and that, most probably, they would pay, or not pay, according to the recommendations I made in my report. Therefore, I said. I'd better have the truth, the whole truth, etc, etc. I added that I would now take a statement from him and that he would sign it when I'd finished. Luckily the gem merchant wrote and spoke English and so there were no complications here. I think if I set out the bones of our conversation in 'question and answer' form it will be easier to read and follow:

Me: 'How did you manage to collect such a large parcel of gems?'
GD: 'I have been collecting this parcel for forty years. We dealers buy parcels of stones from time to time and sell them but we always keep the best stone as 'insurance for our old age'. This parcel was all my

118

best stones collected all my life.'

Me: 'Where did you keep them for all this time?'

GD: 'In that cupboard – it is always locked, there is only one key which I wear on a string round my waist.'

Me: 'What happens to the key when you go to the well for your bath?'

GD: 'It still stays round my waist – it never leaves my waist.'

Me: 'What happened on the day you posted the parcel?'

GD: 'My horoscope said it was an auspicious day so I packed the stones in two packets, star sapphires in one, blue sapphires in the other. I put cotton wool in a cheroot box, wrapped up everything and tacked down the lid of the box and put brown paper, string and sealing wax on the outside.'

Me: 'Who watched you doing all this?'

GD: 'Nobody sir, nobody knew of the stones and I took the parcel myself to the Moratuwa Post Office and sent it to London by registered air-mail – here is the receipt from the post office.'

I asked a lot more questions and the main fact to emerge was that the gem dealer was the only person to handle the stones.

I next went to the GPO in Colombo with the receipt and confirmed that the parcel, intact, had arrived from Moratuwa and had gone on by air to London. By this time I was pretty well satisfied that the steel nuts and bolts were substituted after the parcel left Colombo. And yet I felt I'd missed something. One morning at about 3 am I woke with a start and knew I'd solved the puzzle. I was quite sure the gem dealer had not taken the trouble to weigh the nuts and bolts against 1,800 odd carats of gems if, in fact, he was the culprit. I went to some jewellers in Colombo and found out what 1,800 carats of sapphires would weigh and on checking the postage on the parcel I found out that the old villain had got the right postage for the nuts and bolts but far too much for the gems. The postage had been checked in Moratuwa and again in Colombo.

I sent for the old boy, told him what had happened and said I would give him twelve hours before I called the police. He left my desk without a word. My fees were handsome!

As for the name of my radio play – I called it *Weighed in the Balance*.

About this time Jack Reeves, of whom you've already heard, got engaged to a most attractive Wren Officer called Jean Porter. She was a second officer and had the most beautiful apricot-coloured hair and Reeves was clearly a very lucky chap. They were to be married in Christ Church, Colombo, where Jack's father had been vicar. Jean was to have simply a single bridesmaid in attendance and Jack asked me to be his best man. The bridesmaid was another Wren officer, this time a third officer and her name was Helen and naturally we saw a lot of each other in the time leading up to the wedding. This despite the fact that she was engaged to an RN officer. Having seen Jack and Jean properly spliced, Helen, who was about twenty-two I think, and I continued to see each other quite a lot and she was waiting for her draft to be called for repatriation to England. One day she was frightfully excited and told me that her fiancé's ship was expected in Colombo in a few days' time. I asked who he was, was he a regular RN officer or an 'HO' (hostilities only) and if the latter what did he do in peacetime. Helen said he was an 'HO' and in civilian life he was a rubber planter in Malaya. 'Do you know the name of his rubber estate?' I asked. She did and it so happened that I had heard of it and knew who the Colombo agents were. Without telling Helen I phoned a friend in the agent's office and asked him to tell me about a Commander 'X'. 'Why do you want to know?' said my friend. I told him and he said I'd got the wrong man because Commander 'X' was about fifty-five years old and had two grown-up sons who were also in the Navy and so he was in no position to get engaged to anyone. In fact I *hadn't* got the wrong man and I wished to heaven I hadn't stuck my nose into someone else's affairs. Too late for that and so I broke the news to Helen and I've never been sorrier for anyone in my life. Poor girl, she didn't know what on earth to do and she was naturally dreadfully upset. I suggested she arranged to meet Commander 'X' at the Galle Face Hotel and I would go with her. She would point him out to me and I would ask him what he was playing at.

I asked Helen if she would consider marrying me and, so distraught was the poor child, she said, 'Yes'. Off we went and bought a ring and then I confronted the intending naval bigamist. I introduced myself – 'I'm engaged to Helen and she's going to marry me.' I said. I went on, 'Helen's aware now that you're already married with two sons and she got the information from me – if it's true, you've not behaved too well, have you?' He couldn't have been more at a loss if I'd hit him with his dreaded telescope (had he been carrying it). He asked to be allowed to give Helen dinner that evening, so that he could come clean, and I said I'd no objection if Helen agreed and provided that was the last time I'd ever set eyes on him. Not a nice man.

Helen's draft orders came through all too soon and she departed for England. Things sadly went wrong and after a few months our engagement was broken off and Helen later married a much nicer man.

Still on the subject of Wren officers – but on a lighter note – there was one who used to come regularly to our Jungle School curry lunches and her name was Joan. This little episode therefore goes back about a year. One curry lunchtime I asked Joan whether she would dine and dance with me on the following Saturday at the Galle Face Hotel. She said she would but that she couldn't be ready before 8 pm. 'Why not?' I asked. She looked shifty, guilty and embarrassed – 'Because I'm playing hockey,' she mumbled. 'Don't be disgusting, dear,' I said. 'You're twenty-seven and you can't possibly play hockey at your age – I think it's indecent'. 'You can think what you like,' she said, 'but don't you dare turn up to watch.' Well, of course I did. The Wrens were playing a side of RN officers and in the first half the men were all over the women – figuratively speaking of course. At half time the score was, let us say, 3 – 0 for the RN officers. At the start of the second half

Joan moved up from left back to centre forward, took control of the game and scored seven goals. I was dumbfounded and took her to task at dinner. 'Why didn't you tell me you could play hockey?' I asked. 'I thought you'd 'go off me' if you thought I was a jolly hockey sticks,' she said. 'Where on earth did you learn to play like that?' I enquired. 'I've got two England caps,' she said! Many years later Joan dined with Moose and me and our teenage children in England and then a few years ago Moose and I met her in a shop in Sydney. I'd have made her an admiral if I'd been her boss.

In case you think I did nothing but philander with Wrens, let me assure you I did some work too. I soon became involved completely with my new insurance life at Leechman's and I apparently made an impression on the Colombo insurance world because I was elected to the Committees of the Fire Insurance Association, the Accident Officers Association and the Life Offices' Committee. As you know, I was also Chairman of the Colombo Marine Insurance Agents' Committee. In addition I sat on the Council of the Ceylon Chamber of Commerce, as the member representing insurance interests, and the Chamber appointed me as a marine insurance surveyor and a fire assessor.

I was once asked by a firm of local solicitors to survey and then quote for the fire insurance of the prime minister's private residence. The prime minister was Mr SWRD Bandaranaike, who was later assassinated at the house I was asked to insure. He was the son of the most splendid Ceylonese gentleman, Sir Solomon Dias Bandaranaike, who lived at a place called Veyangoda about eighteen miles from Colombo on the Kandy road. I had passed Sir Solomon more than once, whilst he was on horseback, on my way to and from Kandy and he was always riding an enormous cob rather like, but not quite as big as, a dray horse. I would raise my topee politely and he would respond by raising his crop in a form of salute. Our prime minister was at Oxford where I think he was president of the Oxford Union and I'll tell you later on about the time he lost his temper and threw his tobacco pouch at me. To return to the insurance of his house – I called, by appointment, to inspect the premises so that I could quote a premium for underwriting the risk. I was taken all over the large house in Rosmead Place, some 300 yards from where I lived, and, alas, conditions inside were not quite what I expected and I had to ask for a number of improvements to be made before I took on the insurance. I only mention this small policy because the solicitors told me that Leechman's had been specially asked to quote.

Another risk I was asked to underwrite was unusual, to say the least. The enquiry came from the retired senior partner of one of the two leading firms of solicitors in Colombo. He was a Mr Leslie de Saram and his firm was FJ & G de Saram who had given me the prime minister's house to insure. Mr Leslie de Saram was a great collector of *objets d'art* and he kept a most beautiful home in Colombo filled with wonderful antiques and other treasures. He himself was an impressive figure, tall and slim with a well-trimmed short grey beard – immaculately dressed, he stood very tall and gave one the impression that he was not in the habit of suffering fools gladly. Being a great fool myself I was at pains not to give offence. In fact Leslie de Saram was kindness itself and very amusing – he started off by saying, 'Bayne, I've decided to give a present to the Vatican Museum but as they seem to regard me as the scum of the Protestant faith I don't really know why I'm doing it.' The 'present' was unbelievably lovely and consisted of ninety ivory statuettes of the Madonna which he had collected during his not inconsiderable life. 'What are they worth?' I asked. 'I haven't the foggiest idea,' Mr de Saram replied. 'You tell me.'

Some of the statuettes were two or three hundred years old, they were all carved from solid ivory, they varied in height between ten and twelve inches and, in my view they were priceless. I told Mr de Saram I would have to consult my principals in London for the terms on which they would underwrite the risk. With some reluctance my principals said they would insure the statuettes if they were first numbered, measured, weighed, photographed and then professionally packed under Mr de Saram's supervision. Finally, it had to be understood that no one statuette was deemed to be insured for more than £200, a derisory figure. This was all done and the 'present' was safely and gratefully received by the Vatican.

Another interesting underwriting risk that came my way, although I forget how I got it, was the insurance of the bridge for the film 'The Bridge over the River Kwai'. The bridge, which I am sure you have all seen in the film, was constructed by a local engineering firm and it was immense and would have lasted for hundreds of years had it not been blown up. It had to be strong of course because it carried the weight of a train. The two main risks to be insured were those of flood and premature detonation. The insured value was 700,000 Rs. (£52,500 in those days but only £10,000 today.)

The bridge was built across the Kelani Ganga river in the Kelani Valley near a planting district called Yatiyantota. There is a rest house, at Kitulgala, near the spot where the bridge was located and it was a beautiful setting. The Kelani flowed past the rest house and the water was always a lovely blue-ish green and very clear. The hills were in view and thick jungle covered everything except the tea and rubber estates. Many a happy hour have I spent there listening to the river and jungle noises.

Whilst the filming was going on I met Jack Hawkins and Bill Holden and they were friendly. Alec Guiness, however, seemed to keep himself very much to himself at the Galle Face Hotel and I would often see him there having a drink but usually alone. Many years later Moose and I got to know Jack and Doreen Hawkins very well and dined with them more than once. Many of the extras in the film were friends of mine.

At long last the great day arrived when the bridge was to be blown up. A large number of planters from the area and their wives and others were invited and they were given lumps of cotton wool to stick in their ears. They were seated out of range of the cameras and out of range of flying debris too I imagine. They waited in a fever of excitement – they heard the train coming through the jungle – they saw it reach the bridge – saw it enter the bridge – saw it on the bridge and saw it depart safe and sound into the jungle on the other side. Anti-climax! Scores of little men had to scamper into the jungle after the train and bring it back. It hadn't gone very far because the railway line petered out 100 yards or so into the jungle.

This is what happened – the chief explosives man was stationed in a small shed in full view of the bridge but not in view of the eight movie cameras covering the bridge. In his little cabin the explosives wallah had a console on which eight lamps were mounted. These were all red and each cameraman, as he saw the train approach the bridge and he was ready to shoot, pressed a button and one of the red lights in the cabin turned to green. The explosives man was under strict orders to blow the bridge *only* if all eight lights were green. On the fateful day seven were green and one light was red so he let the train go. It transpired *all* the cameramen were ready, and filming, but a fault in an electrical circuit kept one light at red. It took some days to prepare the whole scene again and this time, with no visitors present, the bridge was blown up as you have all seen.

Towards the end of 1947 Leechman's gave me six months' leave and so I saw England again after a lapse of nine years – a long time. I took my mother with me and deposited her with her sisters in London and found myself a small hotel. Being still a junior in the firm, I was given a winter leave; the 'Burra Sahibs' kept the summer leaves for themselves. And, of course, I was still too junior to warrant an office car and so I had to buy my own. This was a dreary little Ford but at least it was new and gave me no trouble during my six months leave. I took it back with me to Colombo but soon after I got back I traded it in for a second-hand two litre Sunbeam Talbot which was a great little car and quite fast. On two consecutive years I entered for a twenty-four hour reliability trial organised by the Ceylon Motor Sports Club. We left Colombo at 4 pm on the Saturday and had to be back at 4 pm on the Sunday. It was a pretty hairy course, particularly the night bit, and my navigator and I stuffed ourselves with Benzedrine and black coffee throughout to keep awake. The course was about four or five hundred miles in length and, having first taken us to the south of the island, it brought us back along jungle roads and then up 6,000 feet to Nuwara Eliya and home via Kandy. There were secret checks and reversing and other tests en route and I came in second on both occasions. We had only one nasty moment and this was on the second year's trial. It was dawn, pouring with rain and we were coming into Nuwara Eliya where we knew we had a time check and an hour's rest. I was going flat out because we were running a little late (sloppy navigation!) and I was tarting myself up a little to look presentable at the checkpoint. In fact, I was looking into the rear view mirror and combing my hair with both hands off the wheel when my navigator yelled, 'Look out!!' We were pointing into space with a 5,000 foot drop – I ceased my toilette abruptly and hauled the Sunbeam back on to the anything but straight and very narrow road. I would like very much to say that during this dramatic little moment 'I had one eye on the road.' Of course, I can't say that because I have only one eye anyway and that was on the rearview mirror.

I'm supposed to be telling you about my leave in England and here am I digressing as usual. I was now thirty-five and having settled down in London, taken delivery of the Ford and ordered some clothes, I started my leave. One of the early contacts I made was by telephoning Uncle Arthur – you know – the one with the four rows of teeth from my 'little boy' days. I rang through to Hove and got Mary the maid on the line and listened to a long tale of woe. Arthur was not at all well, refused to go to hospital and she, poor old dear, didn't know what on earth to do. I said I'd come down at once and rang off. I'm telling you all this because the end of this particular little episode is interesting, or it certainly was to me.

Mary opened the door to me and I had a shock – she seemed an old, old woman and her uniform hadn't seen a cleaner or a laundry for years. I suppose she was over seventy and, anyway, I hadn't seen her for ages. I went into the house and it was awful – cobwebs everywhere and dust over everything. I went upstairs and there was poor old Arthur in bed. He was grey, his pyjamas were grey, his sheets were grey, everything was grey. Poor old chap, he looked dreadful but managed a wan smile and said hadn't I grown!

I went downstairs and phoned the doctor and asked him why on earth my uncle wasn't in a nursing home. 'He won't go,' said the doctor. I told him to reserve a room in a nursing home and send an ambulance round in an hour. After a mild rebellion I had Arthur downstairs and on his way to a very nice nursing home on the front. When I had had some lunch I looked in on the old man and the change in him was dramatic. He had had a shave and a haircut, he was in clean pyjamas and seemed very cheery. His room looked out to sea and I imagine the sea air by itself was quite a tonic. I went back to London and then called in on Arthur, in Hove, two or three times a week with his mail. He asked me to phone some people and write to others and this I did and he gained in health and strength daily. One day he asked me to bring an old friend of his, George Wilkes, from London and I did this and left the two old boys together chatting quite happily. I called back in an hour or so and had lunch with George Wilkes and then drove him back to St Mary Abbott's Terrace in Kensington. Arthur continued to improve and I kept on going down to Hove but early one morning the hospital matron rang me to say he had died suddenly in the night. I was sad and disappointed to get this news because Arthur seemed to be getting better and stronger day by day. I had just put the phone down when George Wilkes rang to enquire if I had heard the sad news. I said I had and George then asked me if I was aware that he was Arthur's executor and I confessed I did not know this. Anyway, I took George down to Hove again and we arranged the funeral, pensioned off Mary and tidied up Arthur's bits and pieces. We found an extraordinary thing. Arthur had, I suppose, a dozen or so suits and in every waistcoat pocket were little packets of coins. Some had been there so long they were stuck together with verdigris and mildew. He had a horror I understand of being away from the house having forgotten his wallet.

George told me that Arthur had not left me anything in his will because he had lost touch with me completely and had probably even forgotten my existence until the day I visited him in Hove. So George said I was to take anything in the house that I liked and he recommended a picture or two. There were four or five lovely seascapes in the drawing-room and I remembered these oil paintings from my boyhood days. They were all in very heavy gilt frames and I flinched at the thought of trying to get them back to Colombo. So I chose what looked to me like a pewter tankard – it was almost black because it hadn't been cleaned for ages but it had the most attractive shape and it was a full pint pot. George thought I was crazy but after a silversmith had cleaned it for me I discovered it was a George I solid silver mug dated 1716. To finish this anecdote – just before my leave expired, Dorothy Wilkes rang me up and invited me to dinner. I had become great friends with the Wilkeses since Arthur's death and even discovered that Dorothy was my cousin. I arrived at St Mary Abbotts Terrace and whilst we were having a drink before dinner, Dorothy said, 'Alan, George wants to tell you something and I think he's potty to do so and we should let sleeping dogs lie.' (No disrespect intended to Arthur, I'm quite certain.) I was intrigued to say the least and George asked me if I remembered the first day I had taken him to see Arthur in the nursing home in Hove. I said I did. 'Do you know why I was there?' he asked. I said I hadn't the foggiest idea. George said that Arthur was so surprised to discover he had a grown-up nephew and he was so grateful for all I was doing for him that he had sent for George, his executor, and asked him to arrange for a new will to be drawn up at once naming me as the sole beneficiary. Preparation of the new will was in hand but Arthur sadly died before he could sign it.

Arthur left a three-storeyed house in Hove, many treasures inside the house and a sizeable investment portfolio. Under the old will half was to go to the National Lifeboat Institution and the other half to the Dumb Friends' League. George was so cut up at not having the new will ready for signature before Arthur died that he felt he had to tell me the story. I was very glad he did because, though dearly would I have loved that little fortune, I felt happy and proud that Arthur thought well enough of me to have wanted to make me his heir.

This leave was not particularly spectacular but it was nice to meet some more cousins. One was Dorothy Wilkes' sister – Marjorie Bayne – and another was Sybil Bayne, a widow whose husband Gerald was my father's cousin. The Wilkeses were very generous to me by way of hospitality and I was very fond of them. Moose and I still see their son Michael and his delightful wife Audrey.

Marjorie Bayne gave me a very pleasant long weekend once. It was over New Year and she arranged for me to be invited to stay for a few days with Jess and Hereward de Havilland at their charming home in, I think, Hampshire. I motored Marjorie down on New Year's eve and, after tea, I was left to my own devices until it was time to change for dinner. A large dinner party had been arranged for, mainly, the de Havilland test pilots and their wives and this was to carry on until we saw the new year in. Well, it was a black tie affair and things were a bit sticky and staid up to and after dinner. The men were being very modest in their drinking because, they explained to me, it was 'a flying day tomorrow'. However, as the men were sitting over their port someone went to the window and looked out. 'Boys,' he yelled, 'It's snowing!!' This meant there would be no 'flying tomorrow' and then the party took off! Those test pilots really piled on the revs and by the time the 1st of January arrived the noise could be heard for miles around. The next morning Hereward de Havilland and I were sitting in front of a roaring fire sipping brandies and ginger ale, and trying to restore our very poor health, when I asked him if he'd mind telling me about the de Havilland Comet crashes. He said 'not a bit' and proceeded. If you remember, in the late forties or early fifties a number of Comets exploded in mid-air for no apparent reason. Terrorism and hi-jacking were not in vogue then and the explosions were a mystery and, of course, a tremendous worry to all at de Havillands. I had already flown in a Comet to Singapore and this was the first jet and quite the fastest and smoothest aeroplane I had ever been in. They were beautiful aeroplanes and, even better, mine didn't explode.

Well, Hereward started to explain. He said that their back-room boffins had examined as much wreckage as they could lay their hands on and, eventually, they found the cause. I must be careful here to get my facts straight because it was a long time ago and the last thing I want to do is to get anything wrong.

Well, as I recall, Hereward said that the windows in the passenger cabins had moulded plastic frames and the scientists discovered that some window frames had a flaw in the moulding. It was this flaw that gave way when the aeroplane was at a certain height and at a certain speed. Pressure was so great that, when the faulty frames fractured, the aeroplane simply tore itself apart and disintegrated with no time for anybody to send out 'Mayday' or other distress signals.

I asked Hereward how they solved the problem and how they guarded against future repetitions. He asked me if I had ever torn up an old shirt to use as cleaning rags. I said I had. 'What happened when you got to the seam on the shoulder?' he asked. 'I nearly broke my wrist,' I said. 'Exactly,' said Hereward. He went on to explain that the early Comets had a plain stretched skin and that once a window frame gave way the aeroplane simply ripped apart. The new ones Hereward explained, had 'seams' built in to the whole fuselage of the aeroplane in ten inch squares so that, should another window give way, only a small tear would appear and the aeroplane would not disintegrate. It worked, and Comets have been a joy to everyone who has ever flown in them since.

Some years after the de Havilland episode, Marjorie Bayne came out to Ceylon to stay with Moose and me. We took her into a game reserve called Yala in the south of the island and she was thrilled at the animal and bird life she saw. The weather on the last day was atrocious and we had a real tropical cloudburst. I had a largish white Ford Zephyr at the time and we started to make tracks for home. We hadn't gone far, and we were still in the reserve, when the jungle track we were on gave way to a small plain which was flooded. All I could do was to put the Zephyr at the flood and pray hard! We reached the middle and the water was up to the floorboards when the engine gave a cough and packed up. A nasty moment because the flood covered two or three acres of ground, I suppose, and poor Marjorie must have been having a million fits with thoughts of elephants having us at their mercy. I had read in a book once about some character who was stuck in similar circumstances and extricated himself by taking the

130

plugs out of the engine, to remove the compression, and driving the car out of the flood on the self-starter. Out I got, at least it wasn't cold, took out all six plugs and got into the car again, praying very hard by this time! I put the car in first gear and pressed the starter. It worked like a charm and out she came. It was at this point that I went to the back of the car for some rags to dry the engine and plugs when, to my surprise, I saw a large black man sitting on the back seat. I had forgotten all about this character and only remembered then that he had asked for a lift in the jungle before we met the floods. Marjorie, Moose and I had been sitting three abreast on the front seat.

Our adventures for the day were not quite over – as we left the reserve there was a large bull elephant slap in the middle of the road. He was about fifty yards away and looking not best pleased I thought. I brought the car to a smart halt and reversed it across the road so that I could go, at short notice, any way the tusker did not go. We stared at each other for a minute or so and he departed into the jungle. We carried on to our resthouse for hot baths, dinner and drinks – lots of drinks.

All too soon I was back in Colombo to start a fresh three year agreement with Leechman's. Soon after I got back I was made a per-pro for the firm which meant that I held their power of attorney and could sign for the firm. This meant more money too – a good thing.

About this time, say 1948, I joined the Royal Colombo Yacht Club situated at one end of the harbour. Some members had their own smart yachts but the club's fleet consisted of Water Wags, sort of ten feet dinghies with a jib and a mainsail. They also had Sea Birds which were bigger and although rigged the same as the Wags could not be taken out single-handed and it was mandatory to have a crew. Several people took turns in teaching me how to sail and one particular teacher, a married woman called Tege was a scream. She was a fairly tough egg and spoke her mind with no hesitation. Sometimes when she was crewing for me in a race and another crew would make a mistake she would yell, 'That's another stinker out of the race,' or if I would do something silly she'd mutter, 'Stop disgracing me, Bayne.'

131

I enjoyed the years that I sailed but I never enjoyed sailing quite so much as rowing. I sometimes used to sail single-handed and one particular Sunday morning I went down to the club and there was hardly a soul there. It was blowing a half-gale and the boathouse staff were most reluctant to let me have a boat. However, I persuaded them that I knew what I was doing (quite untrue) and they gave me a Wag and off I went single-handed. It was exciting to say the least and the little Wag screamed along like a mad thing. There was a large French passenger liner in harbour that morning, one of the Messagerie Maritime ships, irreverently called Menagerie Maritime, and I decided I'd show off a bit and give the Frogs a lesson in English seamanship, you know, Collingwood and all that. I went round the liner twice and on the third time, like a fool, I managed to get the little Wag jammed against the monstrous hull and the gale kept me pinned quite firmly in place. Much ribaldry from the liner, of course, and a very sheepish Bayne finally got unstuck with the help of a boathook and beat it back to the club.

However, as I say, rowing was my true love and I spent many happy years at the Colombo Rowing Club. We had clinker-built fours (coxed), coxed pairs (also clinker built), and coxless pairs which were racing shells made for us by the Eton boathouse. There were a number of sculling boats belonging to the club and one of the senior members, a Lionel Bray, had his own sculling boat, a wafer-thin shell which he guarded jealously (and quite rightly) and one had to be in his good books and a first-class sculler before one got permission to use it.

We used to have three or four regattas a year and our main race was an annual affair between the Madras Boat Club and ourselves. There was an enormous amount of competition and keenness to be selected for a place in the Colombo boat and some people were so keen they even went on the waggon whilst they were training. Quite absurd. I rowed twice for Ceylon, once at home and once in Madras. The Madras visit was great fun and, in addition to the crew and our cox, we took our sculler Gordon Armstrong of whom you've already heard, the one who tried to assassinate me on four occasions. We started

132

our journey one evening at the Fort railway station in Colombo and caught the night mail to Talaimanar which is at the north-west tip of the island near Jaffna. We were seen off at the station by a large party of oarsmen (*not* in training) and after the regulation Ceylon Government Railway dinner (clear soup, roast chicken and custard pudding) we settled down in our sleepers for the night. At dawn we reached Talaimanar and caught the ferry across the Palk Strait to Danushkodi on the south-east coast of southern India. The ferry crossing was about twenty miles long and the early morning sea was dead calm and a beautiful greenish blue.

At Danushkodi we climbed into our first-class compartments and started our long journey to Madras. As far as I can remember the trip was over twenty-four hours and full of interest. For instance, instead of the lush green paddy fields and thick jungle of Ceylon we looked out to the barren and very hot South Indian Desert. Someone described it as 'miles and miles of damn all with goats eating it.'

It was a non-corridor train and we had to be very nimble at stations because the dining-car and bar were at one end and our compartment at the other. We always seemed to leave the bar at the last moment to sprint along the platform dodging beggars, betel-nut sellers, pi-dogs and goodness knows what else to reach our compartment with the train gathering speed.

We were met at Madras Central station by our hosts for the week we were to spend there and carried off to our various billets having first arranged to meet at the Madras Boat Club that evening for our first outing on the Adyar River.

Gordon Armstrong and I were billeted with the Burra Sahib of Binny & Co. the vast textile firm in south India. Our host was a Mr GR Bambridge – a man of say fifty-five who was kindness itself to us both. He lived in the company house, a vast, beautifully furnished affair with a huge garden and umpteen servants. He put a car and syce at our disposal and merely asked us to let his head bearer know what meals we were likely to be in for each day. 'Gabbo', as he was known to his friends, was a grass-widower whilst Gordon and I were in Madras and so he wasn't behaving too well either.

133

We had two outings a day on the Adyar and it all felt a bit strange to start with because, although we had brought our own oars with us, we used the Madras BC's boats and they all had to be re-rigged to suit us. We had a great time and after our evening outing we would bathe and change and walk over to the Adyar Club or motor to the Madras Club for a few drinks before going home to dinner. Gabbo often joined us and Gordon and I worked on the principle that a little alcohol now and then would do us no harm – or not much. We could have been a bit wrong here because we lost our race and were beaten by Madras by a length.

After the race and after drowning our sorrows at the club we went back to the house and changed into black ties and set off for the Madras Club for the Boat Club dinner. This was a stag affair, very liquid, and it went on for a long time. We rose from table at about midnight and Gordon and I found ourselves at a Red Cross dance – I've no idea how or why. Anyway I met an exceedingly pretty girl and danced with her a lot. I'm a little hazy about how the evening finished but to my great surprise this same girl arrived in Colombo some years later married to a friend of mine called George Bilton. On meeting her I said her face was familiar and I was pretty sure we had met somewhere or other. She said, coldly, she was *quite* sure we had met and proceeded to give me chapter and verse. It seemed I didn't make too good an impression.

We left Madras the next day having had a wonderful week.

The following year Madras visited Colombo and we beat them by four lengths. I rowed at two in the boat again and both crews were quite astonished when we saw each other's coxes. They appeared to be identical twins although they had never seen each other in their lives before.

I was elected captain of the club soon after our race against Madras and had one or two moments of interest. On one occasion we had a visitor from England in the form of Sir Eugene Millington-Drake, an old Oxford rowing blue, I think, and a very keen oarsman. Sir Eugene was our ambassador at Monte Video during the war and at the time of the Battle of the River Plate when the German cruiser *Graf Spee* was lured out to sea and engaged by our cruisers *Ajax* and *Achilles*. *Graf Spee* scuttled herself when she realised it was pointless to carry on the action because she had already been severely damaged a few days before in a monumental battle at sea with Admiral Harwood's fleet of cruisers and destroyers after which she sought refuge at Montevideo on the River Plate.

Anyway, I was asked to lay on a small regatta for Sir Eugene and this I did in the form of one or two races in which fours and pairs took part. After the racing I was entertaining Sir Eugene in the boathouse when he asked me if I was doing anything special that evening. I said no I was not and he invited me to dinner and added it was a black tie affair and would I please be there at 8 pm precisely. The dinner party assembled in the Tudor Room at the Galle Face Hotel and there must have been at least twenty of us in this large and very attractive private dining-room which I knew well. At 8.10 Sir Eugene lined us up and at 8.15 Lord Soulbury, our governor-general, arrived. Now here is the remarkable bit – Sir Eugene had only been in Ceylon for twenty-four hours and knew, possibly, three of his guests for longer than that. He took Lord Soulbury along the line and introduced him to each one of us by name saying who we were and what we did. It was the most impressive display of memory I had ever seen.

On another occasion I had arranged our usual annual North East Monsoon regatta and I was not rowing myself because I had too much to do as we had a full rowing programme. Someone telephoned me at the last moment to say that Ralph Richardson and Trevor Howard were making a film in Ceylon and could they come to the regatta. This was no problem because I had a large launch and crew at my disposal from the Colombo Port Commission and I intended to stick Messrs. Richardson and Howard in that and let them watch the afternoon's racing afloat. How wrong can one be? They duly arrived and I explained that, as captain, I was going to spend the afternoon on the lake and I would be delighted if they would accompany me. 'Do you have a bar?' asked Trevor Howard. I replied that we had a very good bar and I hoped they would see it after the regatta. 'Why don't we go there now?' continued Howard. We did, and although I left them there for the whole afternoon I had to pay them a number of visits to see if they were happy and, in fact, they had a lovely afternoon.

During my many and very happy years at the club I had my fair share of success and have a number of tankards to show for it. I was elected president towards the end of my long sojourn in Ceylon and was still rowing when I left in 1964 aged fifty-two and doing some gentle racing. The five Baynes went back to Ceylon for a short visit in 1976 and one evening we called in at the Rowing Club at about 6 pm. It was strange to see Ceylonese figures draped in towels, as we used to do, having their drinks on the lawn. I walked up to a group and asked if the captain or secretary were there that evening and I was taken to the captain. I introduced myself as a past captain and president and then introduced Moose and our young. The effect was electric and most moving. We were ushered upstairs to the boathouse, given drinks and then taken round to see how many times my name appeared on the record boards.

About this time I was doing quite a lot of commentating for Radio Ceylon. For about ten years on the trot I covered the Caledonian Ball at the Grand Oriental Hotel on 30 November – St. Andrew's Night. My commentary box was placed in a sort of musician's gallery overlooking the combined dining-room and ballroom. The governor-general always attended and I must say it was a spectacular scene with the not inconsiderable number of Scots in Ceylon present in their full-dress regalia. The ladies wore long white dresses with a sash of their tartan, or their husband's tartan, draped across their shoulders. There was always a piper present and after he had piped in the haggis he would march up to the president's table for his customary quaich of whisky. The silver quaich held the equivalent of about three double whiskies and the piper was in honour bound to knock it back in one gulp. I never saw the piper fail but there were times when I suspected I saw a trace of steam coming out of his ears. The snag about these Caledonian Night commentaries was that I had to stay cold sober through dinner and until my hour-long commentary ended at about 11 pm. I usually caught up with the others by midnight. For some days after each commentary a number of up-country Scots would write or ring to say 'thank you' and I was always very touched by this.

I once did a fashion show but disgraced myself by describing a model with a strapless evening gown as 'this beautiful girl with a topless evening gown'. The crowd loved it.

The Queen and Prince Philip visited Ceylon once, in *Britannia*, and I described the docking of that beautiful yacht with the greatest pleasure. It was early morning and the sun shone on *Britannia*'s brilliantly polished dark blue hull as she moored alongside the quay. Her Majesty's standard that flew from the main mast was, someone told me, the size of a tennis court and this I can easily believe. I saw Prince Philip, in his shirt sleeves, on deck chatting to some of the Royal Yacht's officers whilst, below me, the guard of honour was being assembled. The governor-general went on board, and then the Queen and the Duke of Edinburgh came down the gangway, inspected the guard of honour, and drove away in an open Rolls escorted by a squadron of mounted police.

I was presented to Prince Philip the following day when he called on the Ceylon Chamber of Commerce to meet the committee. The greatest honour, for me, was the day after, the Queen's birthday, when I did the commentary for her birthday parade. This was held on the Galle Face green and I suppose some two or three thousand soldiers, sailors and airmen took part. My box was only yards away from the Queen's dais and so I had a marvellous view of her for over an hour. I also did commentaries for President Tito of Yugoslavia, and Prime Minister Nehru of India as well as the very impressive parades held to celebrate VE and VJ days.

I tend to stutter like mad on the telephone so it's strange that I seldom do on the microphone and stranger still that I seemed to have a flair for commentating. Anyway, Radio Ceylon seemed to like it and paid good fees and I enjoyed all my broadcasts enormously.

Radio Ceylon had a charming lady who was head of the entertainment section. Her name was Pearl Ondaatje and we became good friends. She gave me a number of parts in radio plays, some live and some recorded and, off duty, as I say, she was charming. However, when she was on duty rehearsing a play she was a martinet, particularly on the subject of drink. 'Don't you dare have even a sip before you come here,' she used to say. 'I'll detect it in your voice immediately and I'll drop you and rehearse someone else for your part.' After a few radio plays, the president of the Ceylon Amateur Dramatic Club, known affectionately as The Cads, asked me one day if I had ever acted on the stage, I said I had not and she persuaded me to have a go. I was a total disaster. I acted in only two plays and I well remember one critic in *The Ceylon Times*. The play was *The Shop at Sly Corner* by Mary Hayley Bell, I think. Anyway I took the part of the young naval lieutenant and even found a real uniform for the part – medals and all. *I* thought I was very good and eagerly awaited the notices after the first night. *The Times* critic wrote, 'And now we come to a really convincing performance – Alan Bayne as the naval officer was – to the life – Alan Bayne'!! I gave up acting and took to stage directing with more success.

In all I suppose I directed ten or twelve plays at a very good theatre we had in Colombo. It was known as The Lionel Wendt Memorial Theatre after a most charming man of very fine artistic talents. Plays by the Cads usually ran for five or six days and on dress rehearsal night any nurses or members of the armed forces were invited – admission free. They usually proved to be a highly critical, and sometimes vociferous, audience. On opening night the governor-general brought a party and they occupied the front row with HE flanked by the Cads' president and the director of the play.

Of the plays I directed, my favourites were Somerset Maugham's *The Sacred Flame*, Jean Anouilh's *The Rehearsal*, Mary Hayley Bell's *Duet for Two Hands* and William Douglas Home's *The Reluctant Debutante*. We sent Somerset Maugham the notices from *The Sacred Flame* and he wrote us a charming letter congratulating us. Our president pouched this for her collection although I had done all the work!

Duet for Two Hands was a thriller where a famous pianist

damages his hands in a climbing accident in the French Alps and they have to be amputated. A sinister doctor, as a nasty experiment, grafts on a new pair of hands taken from a murderer who had just been hanged. The experiment backfires, however, and the hands, in the last scene, strangle the doctor. Much enjoyed by the audience!

Moose took part in *The Rehearsal* and played Hortentia, a scarlet woman, who seduces the hero to the rage and discomforture of his wife. Moose played this part with such ease and abandon I began to wonder about the wife I had recently married.

A most charming and capable person directed me once in a play; her name was 'Dickie' Allen-Smith and her husband was, I think, auditor general in Colombo. He had had the same appointment in Kenya, I believe, before he was posted to Ceylon. 'Dickie' had the most spectacular head of silver hair – it was quite a feature and one day I remarked on it and said I'd never seen such wonderful and attractive hair. She said, 'It's funny you should say that because five years ago I was as bald as a coot.' I asked her to tell me the story and it was quite remarkable. 'Dickie' said that during their earlier posting in Nairobi some friends came out from England to stay with them. One evening 'Dickie' took the two wives out for a drive after tea. They had a large open car and the three ladies sat in the back with their African driver at the wheel. They had the hood down and were enjoying their drive when they noticed dark thunder clouds gathering in the west. These got closer and closer but 'Dickie' thought they could get home before the obvious deluge and they didn't bother to put the hood up. Suddenly there was a blinding flash of lightning, a simultaneous crack of thunder and an enormous tree beside the road only fifty yards ahead was struck and started to fall. The driver, with great reactions, realised he couldn't stop before the falling tree and so he accelerated as hard as he could. It was a brilliant bit of driving and the car just scraped through with only some light outer branches touching the back of the speeding car. The driver stopped the car and they all looked back in horror at the enormous tree, some thirty or forty yards away, now blocking the entire road. 'Dickie' was sitting between her two guests and they both then had hysterics and were screaming their heads off. 'Dickie' did her best to calm them down but without much success and the two poor dears were still in a great state when they got back to the house. The two ladies went straight to bed where, I have no doubt, a restorative or two relaxed their shattered nerves.

Some months later 'Dickie' awoke one morning to find her bed full of hair. 'This can only be a nightmare,' she told herself, but the hair seemed real enough. She went to her dressing-table and brushed her hair and, she told me, it literally came away with the brush. It was alopecia, brought on by the tremendous shock of the falling tree. Her doctor told 'Dickie' that if she, too, had had hysterics like her two friends she would probably have been all right. It was her courage in bottling up her own terror, in order to calm down her friends, that killed her hair there and then. The story has a happy ending because, as I've said, 'Dickie's' head of hair a few years later was, although silver, a sight to behold.

In the early days of my involvement with the Cads my dear mother resented the whole thing because I was out two or three evenings a week rehearsing. She didn't care for my evenings at the Rowing Club either, in fact there wasn't a lot she *did* care for. This attitude struck me as being unreasonable in the extreme – here she was in a most comfortable home with umpteen servants waiting to ply her with drinks at the raising of a finger and yet I got a rocket for being a little late for dinner. To cap it all my mother used often to say, 'I can't think why you don't get married, dear.' My natural good manners forbade a truthful reply. Imagine such a *menage à trois*. Mercifully, my sister in Singapore finally came to my rescue and suggested she should take over our maternal relative for a year or two. A passage was soon booked, my mother sailed away and I felt like a boy out of school.

Talking of Singapore, I had one or two super holidays there in my sister's lovely house. She and Bill, her husband, were kindness itself and generous to a degree. Hospitality to them knew no bounds and they always gave me a marvellous time.

One morning Phyl, my sister, said, 'I must get on with tonight's party.' 'What party?' I asked. She explained that a few people were dropping in for drinks and to meet me. I asked if it was going to be a big party. 'Not really,' she said, 'about eighty people.' Phyl then went to the telephone and rang the cold stores – she gave her name and said she was having a drinks party that evening for eighty people and would they please organise it. At about 5 pm a van arrived with food, drinks, glasses, waiters and even four syces to drive guests' cars away and park them. It was an exercise in efficiency that I would not have believed had I not been there to see it.

On one visit to Singapore I had an exciting little adventure. I ran into an old Colombo police friend – one Dicky Coombe, now a full superintendent. He said he was organising a bandit raid on one of the islands off Singapore – he would be away for a few days and would I like to come along. I should explain that in the late 40s gangs of bandits were giving a lot of trouble on the Malayan peninsular and, in some cases, they operated from the many islands offshore. I agreed like a shot and we left Singapore in a police launch early one morning with about a dozen police, well armed. On the way we trolled for fish over the stern of the launch with not a lot of success.

In due course we landed on the island and the headman, who was expecting us, met us on the jetty. Dicky and I went to the headman's house and had a palaver with him. Dicky and the headman conversed in Malay and so I didn't understand a word they said. Dicky told me afterwards that he had explained to the headman that he suspected bandits were operating from the island and he would greatly appreciate the old boy's co-operation in rounding them up. He added that he would outline his plan to the headman but that it was of vital importance that the bandits knew nothing of it and that secrecy was the watchword. Wily old Coombe told the headman he was sure the bandits were hiding in the jungle outside the village and so he proposed to seal off the village entirely with his police force and wait for the bandits to make an approach for provisions, etc. He made it clear to the headman where he proposed to have his own police HQ in the jungle and

141

he said he would leave just one gap in the perimeter so that, if necessary, the headman could sneak out at night and bring him any information he could about where the bandits were hiding. Dicky added that the plan was quite foolproof because the headman and he were the only two people who knew where the secret gap in the perimeter was.

Dicky told me that he was positive the headman was hand in glove with the bandits and so he laid an ambush just outside the secret gap. Sure enough – on the second night the headman crept out of the gap and returned with about six bandits, well armed, straight into the ambush. They got the lot.

It seemed to be the custom in Singapore, and elsewhere too I imagine, for an importer to receive gifts every Christmas from his dealers. It was certainly the case with Bill Thurston, my brother-in-law. One Christmas Eve, Phyl and Bill were sitting on their front verandah and dealers were arriving in twos and threes with turkeys, cases of whisky and brandy and other goodies. Two young dealers arrived empty-handed, had a drink with the Thurstons – wished them a happy Christmas and prepared to depart. Bill was unamused and as these two dealers were the last to leave Phyl and Bill accompanied them to their car. They climbed into a large American car leaving a new Morris Minor convertible in the drive. 'Hey,' said Bill, 'Who's going to drive the other car?' 'Oh, Mr Thurston,' they said, 'we quite forgot – that's a little present for Mem Thurston with our best wishes.' Bill was astonished and said, 'We can't possibly accept such an expensive gift.' 'We thought you might say that Mr Thurston,' they said, 'so we hope Mem will use it for a year or two and when it's old she can give it back and we will give her another one!'

Phyl and Bill had a lovely house in Singapore, on a hill not far from the causeway leading to Johore. The garden was a picture and Bill had a passion for orchids – these were so valuable that two Sikh guards watched over them at nights and two *Kabuns* (gardeners) tended them by day. I had more than one very happy holiday with Phyl and Bill and, as I have said, they were kindness itself and hospitable to an extraordinary degree.

142

I propose to digress again for a moment because I've just remembered a strange thing that happened at a party I was once asked to give. Leechman & Co. were chief agents in Ceylon for the New Zealand Insurance Company and as their centenary was approaching they asked me to give a party for 100 guests to celebrate their 100 years of successful underwriting. I had some rather grand invitations printed and these were sent out to the chosen 100. At this time Moose and I had only been married for just less than a year and as she found the Colombo humidity and heat very trying she went to her parents in Sydney to have Julian.

Well, as I was clambering into my black tie, getting ready for the party, the phone rang and one of the guests explained he was in some difficulty because some female friend from up-country had unexpectedly arrived and could he possibly bring her along. I agreed, of course, and the party was a great success until a little drama unfolded right at the end. Everyone had left except for the usual little hard core of drinkers who were difficult to dislodge. In this group was the dreaded woman from up-country whom I had never seen before in my life. She suddenly turned to me and said 'Do you know a man called Alan Bayne?' I said yes I did and why did she ask? She said, 'Well everyone up-country is talking about him and saying what an absolute stinker he is.' 'Why do they say that?' I asked. She said, 'It seems he has met some young girl half his age, put her in the family way and sent her packing to Australia!' Well, as you can imagine, there was a stunned silence in the room and the couple who had brought this harpy to the party, at the last minute, looked at me pleadingly. 'I know Alan Bayne pretty well,' I said 'and you can take it from me that the up-country gossip is rubbish – the girl you talk about is not half Alan's age, he is married to her, they are blissfully happy and she has gone to Australia, to her parents, to have her first, and quite legitimate baby – and now, if you'll excuse me, I have some friends I must take into dinner.' The couple who brought the woman phoned me that night to thank me for letting her down so lightly. I don't know if they ever told her she was talking to Alan Bayne.

143

Now back again to the early 50s because my next home leave was due. This was to be for six months and, as usual, I was given a first-class passage to England and back and full pay, of course.

On board I met a number of Ceylon friends – John and Rae Hampson who managed the Ceylon Brewery in Nuwara Eliya (John did, not Rae!), Freddie Harper and a planter's wife called Margaret Evans. There was also a charming General Evetts on board and we all sat at the same table in the dining saloon and every meal was hilarious.

One day Margaret Evans told me an amusing story. During the war a number of planters sent their wives and children away from Ceylon because the prospect of a Japanese invasion was very real. Margaret's husband, Maurice, sent her off to South Africa for the duration and whilst there she met a very attractive, and un-attached, diamond merchant. They became great friends, saw a lot of each other but, Margaret assured me, there was no nonsense, if you follow me. Well, after a year or so the Japanese scare died down and Maurice cabled Margaret and told her to come home. Margaret broke this news to the diamond merchant who was very unhappy to hear it and he asked if they might have one last dinner together before she left. At dinner the diamond wallah placed a blue velvet box in front of Margaret and in it she found a platinum clasp holding five of the biggest diamonds she had ever seen. 'I can't possibly accept such a very valuable present,' she said. 'Why not?' asked the DM, 'got a guilty conscience?' 'Of course not,' said Margaret. 'Then why not accept the diamonds?' said the DM. 'Put yourself in my husband's position,' said Margaret, 'suppose your wife had been away for two years and came back to you and said she had met a very nice man who had given her a magnificent diamond clasp – what would you think and say?' He said, 'I would say it's a pity they are not bigger diamonds!' She grabbed the clasp!

Margaret told me she had a young daughter in England who was a ballerina in the Sadlers Wells corps de ballet at Covent Garden. She wondered if I would like to go and see her perform one evening. We saw Meriel dance and then I took this very attractive mother and daughter out to dinner at a small theatrical club I belonged to called the Kummel in Burghleigh Street, off the Strand and near Covent Garden and Drury Lane. Meriel was a slip of a girl and I asked her what she would like for dinner. She said, 'A large steak, please.' I knew the Kummel staff very well and I asked for a really large steak for Meriel. An enormous one arrived and Meriel made mincemeat of it. When she had finished I asked her, as a joke, if she would like another one. She glanced at her mother and said, 'I'd love another one – I'm starving!!' I think even a cannibal chief would have been impressed.

During that leave I stayed at a small but very comfortable private hotel in Ennismore Gardens just off the Brompton Road. This was owned and run by a charmer called Rosemary Firebrace who gave me a huge room and private bathroom. No meals were provided and so I skipped breakfast and tea and gave myself a good lunch and dinner – the Brompton Grill was a favourite of mine and so I didn't exactly starve.

During my stay Chez Firebrace I ran into two good friends of mine, Pam and Bob (I will omit their surname). Bob was a tea planter in Ceylon and they too were on leave and staying just outside London. One evening we went to Drury Lane to see *South Pacific* and the lead was taken by Wilbur Evans the American baritone. After the show I took Pam and Bob to the Kummel for dinner and in the middle of our meal the owner of the Kummel, Bobby Page, came up to our table and said 'Alan, how are you getting home tonight?' I said, 'That's a bit hostile – I'm driving home – why do you ask?' He explained that in the last hour a pea-soup fog had come down and visibility was nil – I said my guests and I were on leave, we were in no hurry and so I would be driving home. He said, 'Good, will you please drop Wilbur Evans off at his flat in Berkeley Square?' I said I would with pleasure and off we all went to where I had parked my car. The fog really was thick but I knew my London pretty well and off we started. Pam was sitting next to me in front and Bob and Wilbur were squeezed into the back. After a few minutes Bob turned to Wilbur and said, 'Mr Evans, in *South Pacific* you take the part of a French planter – I'm a tea planter from Ceylon – I plant tea – what are you supposed to be planting?' Wilbur scratched his head and said, 'You know, Baab – I'm goddamned if I know!!' It made our evening.

Bob sadly died a few years later at a comparatively young age and left poor Pam to become a very young widow. Some time later she became friendly with an elderly Frenchman who treated her abominably and one night, somewhere in the South of France, he had had too much to drink and was tormenting Pam past the limit of her endurance. She hit him with a champagne bottle and killed him. Pam, being a thoroughly honest person, took a plane to England and gave herself up to the police. She went to gaol for many years poor dear. They said at the time that had she gone straight to the *French* police and explained the circumstances of the killing they would have treated it as a *crime passionel* and let her off with a scolding.

Another uncle of mine died during this leave and one day I telephoned his widow in Cornwall to ask if there was anything I could do to help. She said there were one or two things that were worrying her and could I come down for a night or two so that we could chat. I drove down in my Minx Convertible (a most boring barouche – I can't think why I ever bought the dreaded thing) and finally arrived at Aunt Ag's cottage. This was a charming house on a small hill above the Helford River with glorious views all round. On the opposite side of the river was the Ferryboat Inn where AP Herbert used to spend a lot of time. I had a very happy couple of days and sorted out a few problems for Aunt Ag. As I was getting ready to return to London Aunt Ag said, 'Alan, I'm afraid your Uncle Charles left you nothing in his will but there is something here which I think you might like and I know he would have loved you to have.' I mention here, purely in passing, that the late Uncle Charles was the elder brother of Uncle Arthur who left all his money to a cat's home! Anyway, I was eager to know what the 'something' was Aunt Ag was going to give me. She went off and came back staggering under the weight of a guncase. This was very dusty but it was a lovely case. 'I don't know what the gun is like, dear,' said Aunt Ag, 'but I know your Uncle loved

146

it and used it a lot.' I undid the straps and opened the lid – there, pasted on the red baize was a label which read 'Holland and Holland'. I couldn't believe my luck and was even more delighted when I took out a Holland 'Royal'. I used that beautiful gun for many years and many were the snipe, duck, pea-fowl and jungle fowl that paid the price of Uncle Charles's generosity.

When we were engaged in 1958, Moose and I went to see Aunt Ag who was by this time living in a hotel in Surrey. She had contracted Parkinson's disease, poor dear, but this had done nothing to diminish her sense of humour. She said to Moose, 'I'm sitting on my hands dear because they shake so much if I don't.' When we told Aunt Ag that we were engaged she looked at Moose and said, 'I think you'll be all right dear – a Bayne never ill-treats his guns or his boats!' As we were leaving she offered a final word of advice, 'To get your way with a Bayne, dear, approach him with a lump of sugar in one hand, and have a riding crop behind your back, in the other.'

During this leave my ex-jungle school adjutant, Roy Webber and his wife Sheila were home on leave too and had rented a very nice house in Sydney Street off Exhibition Road. In fact, Roy met me at Tilbury and took me off the ship and on the way to my digs in Ennismore Gardens he stopped near the Ritz. He explained he had to pop into Fortnum's to buy a cake for some bun-fight Sheila was giving. I went in with him and he parked me in Fortnum's restaurant and said he would be back in a few moments. Well, I sat there happily staring around at London people for the first time in three years when suddenly a most beautiful woman walked up to me, smiled, opened her coat, did a pirouette and swept off. A minute later another gorgeous lady did the same thing. I nearly had a fit and was so embarrassed I didn't know where to look, when suddenly I spotted bloody Webber doubled up with laughter about three tables behind me. It was, of course, a mannequin parade and the evil Webber had parked me in the middle of it on purpose to see how his late commanding officer would react in a real emergency!

The Webbers and I had great fun on that leave and they

147

were kindness itself to me. (I was kindness itself to them too!) We did a lot of shows together, motored about the countryside and had a great time. Roy had an identical Hillman Minx Convertible to mine and in this one day we visited their young daughter Carolyn who was having a camping holiday at a place called Fingering Ho. I used to embarrass them by pretending I thought it was called Fingering Who?

One day Roy and I took ourselves off to the Tower of London because I hadn't been there since I was a little lad. We arrived in time to see the old Tower guard being dismounted and the new guard mounted. On that day guard duties were in the hands of the 2nd Coldstreams I think. They were known, affectionately, in India, as the Tunda Pani Chowkidars – literally 'cold water watchmen'. Anyway, the old guard, now dismounted, had been sloppy or something because their officer was livid with them and was telling this party of guardsmen exactly what he thought of them in no uncertain terms. We could only see his nose and cheeks under his bearskin and these were purple with rage. He was shouting and yelling so much Roy and I thought he would burst a blood vessel at any moment. 'What an angry old man,' said Roy. The incensed officer dismissed the guard with a final volley of abuse and his orderly approached with his cap to replace his bearskin. The irate officer removed his bearskin and Roy and I nearly had a fit. He could not have been more than nineteen or twenty years old!

As usual, my leave came to an end all too soon and I found myself on the boat train to Liverpool to catch the Bibby liner MV *Derbyshire* back to Colombo. The dreaded Hillman Minx was on board too but I knew she would not be mine for much longer because I was determined to swap her for something else as soon as I got back. One of the cars in Colombo that I had long admired was a two and a half litre Riley belonging to the head of George Stewart and Company. His name was Ham Gourlay and the car was one of the nicest looking saloons I had seen and was finished in a metallic sea-green colour with matching green leather upholstery inside. As luck would have it Ham's wife, May, was also travelling in the *Derbyshire* and

148

one day I told her about the Minx and that I planned to part with it as soon as possible. I added that the car I really admired was Ham's Riley and she said that, although it was easy for Ham and their driver to handle, it was too long and heavy for her to drive on up-country roads. 'I think Ham might be ready to sell if he got a good offer,' said May. Well, a cable was on its way to Ham within the hour and the Riley was mine before we docked in Colombo. I've got a photograph of her somewhere so I hope you'll see how nice she was.

Back I went to my little bungalow Shalimar to a great welcome from my servants and my dear old pi-dog, Stinky. Back I went to Leechman's and by this time I held their power of attorney and signed 'per pro' for the firm.

One day I was called into the partner's room with Mac Bartlett, our tea expert and the father of the little boy who, if you remember, was bitten by a snake one Sunday morning. Bartlett and I had the same seniority in Leechman's and we both sat down facing the partners and wondering what was coming next. They explained that the senior partner of the legal firm who handled Leechman's business was about to retire and had indicated that he would like to *buy* a partnership in Leechman's. 'Buy' is the operative word because a partnership in the firm had never been 'bought' before – they were always given in recognition of one's service. Our partners went on to say that the gentleman in question, who would be senior to us, was a Ceylonese, a man of considerable legal and business ability, educated in England and fifty years old, a good deal older than Bartlett or me. They added that Stanley de Saram was going to be a great asset to the firm and they hoped very much that Bartlett and I would understand the circumstances of de Saram's partnership and not feel hurt or overlooked. They assured us that our partnerships would come in due course in the usual way. We met Stanley de Saram a few days later, liked him, and I little realised then that the de Saram family would become Moose's and my great friends until they died. More of this anon. Bartlett and I said we agreed to the Partners' wishes.

By the time Stanley was fifty-one he had been to the Rowing

Club as my guest and one day he asked me if he could become a member. As it happened, we had just decided to admit carefully chosen Ceylonese as members and Stanley was an obvious choice. He brought a friend, another Ceylonese and an ex-partner of his from his old legal firm to meet the committee and they were elected together. Stanley's friend was another charming man called David Maartenz, also fifty-one years old, and I taught them both how to row. One day they shyly gave me a lovely old silver tankard inscribed 'Thank you – 102 not out.'

About this time I met a character called Mike Henderson, a younger man than me and with two great attributes – he was a good shot and an even better golfer. He was an impertinent young man – he used to call me 'Molesworth'. 'Why Molesworth?' I asked him one day. 'Because you look like a Molesworth,' he replied. I said, 'Thank you very much.' One day Mike asked me if I had ever played golf – I said I hadn't because I really hadn't the time. I explained that what with rowing, swimming, diving, sailing, thespian activities and, now and again, a little work – I was, I felt, fully occupied. 'Rubbish,' he said (I told you he was most impertinent) and one Sunday afternoon he took me to a little used bit of parkland and began to explain the rudiments of the great game. He had brought his caddy and his clubs and he demonstrated the stance, the grip and, roughly and briefly, the swing. He hit a few balls, handed me an iron and said, 'Now you have a go.' 'Beginners' Luck', call it what you will – but I managed to hit a few not unreasonable shots and I think the dreaded bug bit me that afternoon. I now love the game deeply and play whenever I can.

You will remember that I now had my shotgun and, this having been thoroughly overhauled by Holland and Holland, I was ready and eager to go into action. It soon became an established routine that every Christmas and Easter Mike and I would depart for some place towards the east coast where we had information that the snipe, duck and jungle fowl were plentiful. We would always travel in Mike's little open Fiat Topolino (little mouse) because it would go down almost any jungle track it was so small. A typical day went something like this: — the resthouse keeper would bring us our early morning tea at 5 am and by 5 30, and still dark, we would set off in the little Fiat, and with the hood down, for some jungle tracks we knew well. We had already tossed up as to who would drive and who would stand up with the gun. The driver had a cricket stump by his side and I will explain this odd piece of equipment in a moment. By first light we had reached our jungle track and proceeded to motor down it as quietly as possible. Now, jungle fowl get pretty wet with dew in the jungle overnight and at dawn they move out on to a track to have a bit of a chat and dry off. What the poor creatures didn't realise was that Henderson and Bayne knew all about their little habits. Round a corner we would come and, sure enough, there would be eight or ten jungle fowl right in the middle of the track gossiping away. The driver would slow the Fiat and the 'gun' would fire off both barrels into the middle of the pack. The driver would then smartly stop the car, taking care not to decant the 'gun' over the windscreen, grab the cricket stump and dash into the group of jungle fowl despatching any which were only wounded. We usually got two or three birds and we would then go back to the resthouse, give the birds to the cook and order jungle fowl curry for lunch. We would then shave, have our baths at the resthouse well and sit down to a hefty breakfast. Jungle fowl are smaller than our cocks and hens and more brightly coloured, in fact not unlike our bantams. Delicious in a curry and, of course, the resthouse staff were only too happy to eat most of our lunch knowing there would be a fresh supply in the morning.

After breakfast we would laze around until about 11 am, when the sun would be getting really hot, and the snipe a little sleepy, and then we would go to various villages where there were plenty of paddy-fields. At this dry time of the year the paddy-fields were not in cultivation and snipe abounded in them because just under the fairly hard surface there was thick swampy mud teeming with insects which snipe, with their long bills, could easily dig out. In the two rice seasons every year, during the rains, the villagers would plough their paddy-fields with buffaloes and these were then let loose in the surrounding jungle to forage for themselves in the dry seasons. Consequently the buffaloes were almost wild when we were shooting snipe and they have been known to charge one. Not funny. Mike and I usually got thirty or forty birds each every morning and these we would take back to the resthouse and pack them into the large teak ice-box we brought with us.

At about 2 pm we would have lunch and then sleep until about 4 pm or so when, after tea, we would go out after duck. I liked this part of the day best when, standing up to one's waist in a tank (a large fresh water lake), the duck would come flighting in at dusk. One's first shots were always a surprise because one had forgotten the considerable muzzle flash a twelve bore has when fired at night.

I say I like duck shooting best – well, there was one occasion when the attraction palled pretty smartly. The sun was beginning to set and I was standing up to my waist in water with my cartridge belt round my neck. I had my tracker, a young Tamil boy, by my side and he was swimming out into the tank to bring in any duck I shot. Suddenly I noticed movement in the reeds in which I was standing, about ten feet away. I said to my young tracker, '*In-na*?' ('What's that?') '*Motherly dorai*,' he said. ('Crocodile'.) I then saw it, a fairly large one, and lost all further interest in duck shooting, standing in water, for that evening. Henderson, on the other side of the tank, was blissfully unaware of my little drama and couldn't understand why I was shooting from the bank.

On one occasion Mike arranged for an elderly widower friend from England to spend two nights with us at the resthouse. The friend was accompanied by his not unbecoming daughter, Charlotte, and on the first evening we went off on our duck shoot. When we got to the tank Mike went to the far side with his friend whilst Charlotte came with me. I explained to Charlotte that I was going to wade into the tank up to my waist and would she like to come? She decided, forcibly, that she would not but said that if I would carry her out to a small island in the tank, about fifty yards away, she would like to sit there and watch. I hoisted her on to my shoulders, with my cartridge belt round *her* neck because she complained it was uncomfortable to sit on. (Some women!) Off we went and I duly deposited her on her tiny island. Before I left, I asked Charlotte if she would be very kind to me when we got back to the resthouse, cosset me and generally do anything I asked. 'Why should I agree to all this?' she asked testily. 'Because I'm going to damn well leave you on this island if you don't,' I said. She was very sweet.

In Colombo I was involved in an entirely legal and unofficial association, with some others, and we were trying to do what we could to protect British interests in the island. The authorities got wind of our existence and the prime minister summoned three of us to his office to find out what was going on. We duly presented ourselves before Mr Bandaranaike who was seated at his desk smoking his pipe. He asked us a lot of questions and seemed to get crosser and crosser at our answers. Finally he said if we continued with our activities he would withdraw our passports. I was getting cross by this time too and I said if our passports were confiscated the British press would love it. This proved too much for the PM – he picked up his tobacco pouch and flung it at me missing me by inches. We left and heard no more.

The rest of my three year agreement proceeded calmly and without incident and I began counting the days before my ship would arrive to take me on another leave. Finally the great day arrived and my head boy – Appu – having packed my bags for me took them on board the *Chusan*, a P & O liner, met my steward and un-packed for me. He then came ashore and I went on board at about 6 pm straight from the office. They made you work in Leechman's. We sailed, as usual, at midnight, and another marvellous leave began. Actually it began before we sailed because I had invited one or two friends on board for dinner and so I wasn't at my best the next morning.

I've just thought of something else that happened to me some years earlier. Returning from a leave on an Orient liner – the *Orion* – I got to know a charming and very pretty purserette on board. She used to ring me up whenever the *Orion* called at Colombo and we would have dinner together at the Galle Face

Hotel or Mount Lavinia or somewhere. After one of these visits I was seeing this girl back to the *Orion* and our launch tied up against a pontoon which was moored to the side of the ship. I was saying goodbye at the foot of the gangway when some friends in the launch yelled at me to say the launch was leaving and was in fact already under way. After one hurried peck I sprinted across the pontoon and leapt for the launch which was now almost six feet away. I landed on the small side deck and grabbed for the handrail on the roof – missed, and went straight into the harbour. I remember the phosphorescence under the water from the twin screws of the launch as it went past me. The launch circled, came back and fished me out of the harbour to the wild cheers of those passengers looking down from the ship. The customs officers and other officials were highly amused at this bedraggled creature squelching his way along the passenger jetty.

Now, back to the *Chusan* and my leave. Nothing much happened on the voyage home and on landing at Tilbury I was met by friends who very kindly motored me to Sharpthorne in Sussex where I was booked into a small and very comfortable hotel recommended to me by a tea planter friend. The friends who met me at the ship were Norma and David Hutcheson in their MG Magnette and one of the reasons for their kindness was that David and I, together with another friend, a wild banker called John Wichers (pronounced 'Vickers') were going to enter for the Monte Carlo Rally. John Wichers also had a Magnette and I was taking delivery of mine in a few days time from the factory in Abingdon. So we were all set for the Monte Carlo Rally until it came to the crunch – whose Magnette would we use? There were no volunteers and we withdrew our entry!

The hotel I stayed at was called Old Plaw Hatch, which is Anglo-Saxon for 'a gap in the forest', and it was situated in the middle of Ashdown Forest near the village of Sharpthorne. It was a lovely old house and the owner, Kathleen Batten, was kindness itself. I was given a nice bedroom with a bathroom en suite and so I could not have been more comfortable. Kathleen Batten had a niece known as 'Totty' and she was the most beautiful creature, about twenty-five years old and with a face and figure that would have made many a catwalk lady green with envy. During the week the hotel was not very busy and sometimes at lunch I would be the only one in the dining-room with the whole staff waiting on me. Kathleen had the endearing habit of calling everyone 'Sweet' and whilst I came in for my fair share of 'Sweet' her niece called me Earl Grey because I was connected with the tea business. I put on a lot of weight at Old Plaw Hatch and whenever I said 'no' to pudding after a large main course Kathleen would say, 'Oh go on, Sweet, – at least have a look at it!'

After a day or two John Wichers called round and we went up to Oxford by train to collect my Magnette from the MG factory at Abingdon. She was ready when we arrived and she was finished in black with green upholstery. I drove John back to Sussex very carefully because I had given us both a very good lunch at The Randolph in Oxford before we collected the car. I think I've already said that I saw 'Emma' again in Sri Lanka after a lapse of thirty-five years with over 500,000 miles on the clock.

It was mid-winter when I was at Old Plaw Hatch and it snowed a lot that year. I remember some of my afternoon walks in Ashdown Forest with thick snow everywhere and it was all very beautiful and quite a contrast to Colombo in December. There was a marvellous old pub not far away called The White Hart and originally it was the hunting lodge of Charles II I believe. It had a mantrap over the front door and this was the most fearsome device and the first one I had ever seen. Gamekeepers certainly meant business in those days. Totty and I, and others, used to motor over to The White Hart after dinner sometimes, or before lunch on Sundays, and it was all great fun. Breathalysers were not invented then.

At weekends a lot of interesting people used to come down from London and the pace used to quicken considerably. Once or twice Kathleen would say to me, 'Sweet, are you staying in this evening?' When I said I was she would say, 'Oh Sweet, would you be very sweet and do an hour behind the bar after dinner?' This was always good fun and I loved it when strangers would offer me a drink or a tip after I had served them.

One couple I grew very fond of was an actress called Mary Mackenzie and her stockbroker husband, Anthony Sewell, and more of Anthony anon. Then there was a regular visitor, who shall be nameless or shall I call him 'Fred'? 'Fred' was madly in love with Totty and this did nothing to endear him to me. He was a nice enough chap, immensely rich, but with a very dodgy nasal organ. This was almost continually dripping the most sinister-looking drips or, when dry, he would be for ever exploring the not inconsiderable interior with a grubby forefinger. He had a lovely Lagonda which made my MG look very feeble indeed and so did a stream of the most beautiful Jaguars brought down from time to time by Duncan Hamilton, the well-known Jaguar driver and dealer.

One Saturday evening, after dinner, three guests came up to me and asked if I played poker? I said yes I did and they invited me to make up a four. I did quite well for half an hour or so, very well in fact, when Totty came up to me and said Colombo was on the line and they wanted me urgently. I threw in my hand and followed Totty. 'Thank goodness I saw you,' she said, 'that's a professional poker school from London and they've got your measure – they'll clean you out – please go to bed and don't come down again – I'll make some excuse for you.' Good old Totty. One last word on Old Plaw Hatch – it was just before Christmas and my bonus had come through from Leechman's and so I was feeling no pain. I bought Totty a gold compact as a Christmas pressy and I gave it to her at breakfast. Fred, 'the nose' came down at lunchtime from London – empty-handed – and I thought this would dish his chances with Totty in no uncertain terms – not so, alas! There was a sudden clattering in the yard outside and there was a groom leading the most lovely chestnut hunter – 'Totty – with love from 'Fred'.' Oh well – you win some and lose some.

All too soon I was back at my desk at Leechman's and settling in for another agreement – this time for only two and a half years. The year was 1955 and I was forty-three.

9

1955 – 1958
Last Bachelor Years and the Advent of Moose

The following year Bartlett and I were made partners in the firm and I felt very grand. I now had only to keep an eye on the insurance department and to concern myself more actively in Leechman & Co's main business of tea and rubber. I was given three tea companies and two rubber companies to run and they comprised about sixteen or seventeen estates in total. I loved it, particularly when it came to visiting 'my properties' up-country. The planters were very kind to me in the early days when they realised I could barely distinguish a tea bush from a rubber tree and they taught me a lot.

During this agreement and my last as a bachelor – although I didn't know it at the time – I found myself to be a director of a number of tea and rubber companies, The Ceylon Brewery, The Ceylon Gas Company, Ceylon Re-diffusion, an Insurance Company, Chairman of the Colombo Marine Insurance Agents Association, Deputy Chairman of the Fire Insurance Association, insurance representative on the Ceylon Chamber of Commerce Committee, President of the Colombo Rowing Club and President of the Ceylon Amateur Dramatic Club. So I wasn't exactly idle.

On the domestic front there were three little incidents I'll always remember. Some great friends, Reggie and Bene Bois were giving a dinner party. Bene told her cook she wanted to serve dressed crab as the first course so he was to get on his bicycle and go to the fish market for the crabs. She warned him

157

that they were to be alive when he bought them and that as soon as he got back she was to be called to see the crabs to be sure they *were* alive. Bene was duly called and she went out to the kitchen to inspect the cook's purchases. On an old gunny bag on the floor was a green mound of very moribund crabs – dead as doornails. 'Cook – these crabs are dead,' said Bene. 'No Lady – not dead,' said cook. 'I tell you they're dead,' said Bene. Said cook, 'not dead Lady – simply tired after the bicycle ride!'

The other incident concerned more friends – this time Taffy and Ethel Lloyd. Their cook took a great delight in decorating ice puddings he used to make for dinner parties and sometimes he went too far with his ornamentation. Before one important party Ethel warned him to go easy on the decorations, 'Just something simple, Cook,' she said. Time for the pudding arrived and Cook produced his masterpiece and showed it to Ethel first for approval. On the top in half-inch print, in cochineal, were the words 'Made in England'.

The last incident happened to me: I was giving a dinner party and it was an important one – a black tie affair. A very sweet girl called 'Birdie' Kenyon had agreed to act as my hostess and I sent my car to bring her to my house in good time. I gave her a drink and whilst she was sitting on the sofa sipping it I sent for my head boy and gave him some last minute instructions and then I sent for my second servant and told him something or other. I then checked the drinks table, the dining-table and fluffed up a cushion or two. Birdie watched all this, called me over to sit beside her, patted my knee and said, 'Alan, one day you're going to make someone the most marvellous wife!'

After I had been back in Colombo for a few months I had a letter from Anthony Sewell. I had met him at Old Plaw Hatch with his actress wife, Mary MacKenzie, if you remember. Anthony said a very good client of his – the Hon. Sylvia Henley – was going to spend two weeks in Colombo as the guest of our prime minister – (not 'tobacco pouch' Bandaranaike) Sir John Kotelawala. As she knew no Europeans in the island, Anthony asked if I would please make myself known to her and perhaps

158

give her dinner one evening. He added a postscript to his letter – a postscript mark you – 'Mrs Henley is accompanying her sick cousin, Clementine Churchill, who is to convalesce in Ceylon.' The ship was due in on a Saturday morning and I sent a letter on board with our high commissioner, Sir Cecil Syers. In the letter I introduced myself to Mrs Henley, said I was at her service, gave my office and home telephone numbers and said I hoped I might give Lady Churchill and herself dinner one evening. We used to work half days on Saturdays in those days in Colombo and so I knocked off at 12.30 or so and went home and started on my first pink gin before lunch. I knew I would not hear from Mrs Henley until the following week at the earliest and so I was pretty relaxed. I had had only two sips or so of my pink gin when the telephone rang. A voice said, 'This is the prime minister's residence – Mrs Henley wants to speak to you.' She came on the line – seemed very pleased with my letter and said, 'You did say, Mr Bayne, that my cousin and I could dine with you one day – shall we say this evening?' Without having a clue as to how I was going to cope I said, 'Of course, I'm delighted – I'll be wearing a black tie and will it be all right if I call for you at 8 pm?' It was agreed, and then I sent for Appu, my head boy, and said I knew the shops were shut on Saturday afternoons but what could he give us for dinner? Not a lot I gathered from his reply and so I rang my most dear Aimée de Saram and said, 'Aimée, would you like to give Lady Churchill dinner this evening?' As soon as Aimée realised I was not joking she sprang to my rescue and she said, 'Alan, you bring your ladies here at 8.15 and we'll be ready.' What a relief! Well, I was at Temple Trees – the PM's residence – at 8 and I was ushered upstairs to the ladies' private drawing-room. It was a great thrill to see this famous figure walk across the room to greet me. We went downstairs to my gleaming car and Lady Churchill said, 'Oh Sylvia – what a super car – look, I'll sit with him going and you can sit with him coming home!' We arrived at The Eyds, the de Saram's lovely home, and there were some white-coated servants waiting for us. Aimée and Stanley were on the verandah and I presented my guests. At one stage I lived alone at The Eyds for six weeks, whilst the de Sarams's were on leave, and so knew just how grand it was. They had thirteen servants, the most beautiful antique furniture, rugs, silver, paintings and, in addition, Stanley had a cellar of lovely French wines – he was a great connoisseur.

We sat down in the drawing-room and Stanley asked the ladies what they would like to drink. He was ready, I knew, with everything from French champagne downwards. 'Some lime juice perhaps, Mr de Saram? said Mrs Henley. Stanley's face fell and I could see him thinking that if his two guests stuck to lime juice for the whole evening, dinner was going to be hard work and his lovely wines would not be appreciated. Aimée realised that dinner would need to be brought forward by an hour at least and so urgent signals were sent to the kitchen. We sat down to dinner and with a feeling of despair Stanley turned to Lady C and said, 'A little sherry perhaps!' 'Oh yes, please,' said Clemmie and so did Sylvia. To cut a long story short, those two ladies knocked back glass after glass of everything Stanley had to offer and dinner was a great success. It was just that they didn't drink before dinner.

Lady Churchill couldn't travel because she was convalescing and so I took Sylvia Henley up-country for a few days. While we were away Aimée 'mothered' Clemmie and they became firm friends, so much so that the following year, when the de Sarams were on leave, they lunched with the Churchills at Chartwell and Aimée sat on Winston's right. She told me afterwards that he tended to nod off towards the end of lunch after about his tenth brandy.

I took Sylvia Henley to Roy and Sheila Webbers' tea estate called Fordyce in the district of Dikoya. Well, the estate was just very good – it was the house and garden that were lovely. All went well until the last morning when Roy (he was my jungle school adjutant if you remember) took us to see his crèche of which he was most proud, and quite rightly. All the attendants were on parade and the little girl babies had pink rubber sheets and the boys blue. It was, of course, an estate crèche for the use of the Tamil labour force but it was well organised, spotlessly clean with a medical officer in charge.

160

Roy and I both gained the impression that Sylvia was looking down her nose at the crèche and then she made an unfortunately inapt remark about crèches in England and how very good they were. Roy drew himself up to his full height (he was six foot three inches) and said coldly, 'Perhaps, Mrs. Henley, if you saw the conditions in which these people normally live in their villages in south India you would not be so critical.' There was an ugly silence!

One evening I took both ladies to a play directed and acted by Sinhalese. The theme was political and a good deal of skulduggery, bribery and corruption took place. It was very well done and my guests were highly amused. As we were leaving the theatre I asked Lady C if she had enjoyed it. 'Very much, Alan,' she said, 'although I don't think my husband would have cared for some parts of it!' I could well imagine this.

The fortnight passed all too quickly and I saw both ladies off aboard their ship. Lady Churchill wrote me two most charming letters from the ship and from England and Sylvia did too. Some years later Sylvia invited Moose and me to tea at her flat in South Kensington – 'Tea is at five,' she said, 'don't be late.' We were late and got a rocket! On leaving she gave me an awfully nice paperweight of black agate inlaid with flowers which I still have on my desk.

As we were leaving Sylvia's flat we ran into Jack Hawkins and his wife Doreen and I was able to introduce Moose to Jack. We met them again at dinner on two occasions at Bene and Reggie Bois's flat and the second time was sad because, by then, Jack's throat cancer was very bad.

Shortly before my next leave was due I was asked by friends in England to meet a young girl who was passing through Colombo on her way to Australia to marry a young man she had met in London. Her name was Jenny Crooks and she was twenty-one. She telephoned me from the general post office in Colombo just as I was about to leave the office. I picked her up, gave her a short tour of Colombo and drove her home to have a drink whilst I bathed and changed. We had dinner at the club and then I saw her back on board her ship. Jenny was a very

161

lovely young thing and so smitten was I that I told myself sharply to remember she was then less than half my age. Jenny married a most eligible young man called Ion Macarthur-Onslow and we are all great friends and see each other in Sydney, or in Sussex, every year.

Some time before I met Moose there was another case of the Sinhalese and Tamils being at each other's throats. The troubles seemed to have been centred round Colombo and tempers were running pretty high. Our tea and rubber stores were some ten minutes drive from our offices and our labour force consisted largely of Tamils. These people blended tea – a fascinating sight of a pyramid of black tea some twelve feet high surrounded by ten or twelve workers with large wooden spades shovelling up the black tea from the bottom of the pyramid and heaving it on to the top. The blend would consist of say six or eight different sorts of black leaf from various estates and the labourers' job was to mix it up as I've described. The work force also assembled tea-chests and lined them, and packed them, and in another part of the stores other labourers dealt with the stocks of rubber we held awaiting shipment.

Well, one evening I was just getting ready to go home when one of the partners came up to my desk and said there was trouble at the stores and would I go and sort it out. He almost said, 'I want one volunteer – you, Alan.'

Down I went and, although the lane leading to the stores was pretty peaceful, the main road, from where the lane started, was a seething mass of Sinhalese yelling and shouting and working themselves up into a great state. They had surrounded the two or three buses we had hired to take our Tamils home. I drove into our stores and asked the storekeeper what the trouble was. He said the labourers were frightened to leave the store and go to their buses because of the horde of angry Sinhalese waiting outside to beat them up. I personally seemed to be on a hiding to nothing and my strong inclination was to tell them to spend the night in the store. However, I felt that that was too easy an option and that I'd better display some qualities of leadership which I certainly did not feel.

162

I told the storekeeper to get the whole gang lined up with their things ready to go to the buses. When this was done I told them that they must follow me closely and I would lead them safely to their buses. I explained that the Sinhalese would not dream of attacking them whilst I was there – (Ha! Ha! Ha! how silly can one get?).

Well, the fifty or so labourers fell in behind me, the store gates were thrown open, and with a last injunction to stay close to me, I led my little band into the lane. On seeing us the crowd went quite quiet and just stared. 'Good show,' I thought to myself, 'it's going to work.' We had progressed some fifty paces up the lane, my bare-footed followers quite silent behind me, when the Sinhalese suddenly burst into howls of laughter. I wondered what on earth had amused them. Were my flies undone? Was my fear showing? What was causing the merriment? I looked round – there wasn't a labourer in sight – they had all fled back to the stores as soon as they saw the size of the crowd. I threw up my arms in despair and walked back to the stores to the cheers of the now quite friendly Sinhalese.

By this time I was a partner in Leechman's, as you know. I was also a director of umpteen companies, I was still doing my marine survey and fire assessing work, and so the rupees were pouring in. Now they say that in spring a young man's fancy turns to love – well, this (comparatively) young man's fancy turned to Bentleys. You see, being a partner in Leechman's, I had an office car and driver and I was to buy another car in England, to use during my leave, and then ship back to Colombo. This was to be another MG Magnette (all Leechman's would allow) and so I saw no good reason why I shouldn't have my private automobile as well and what could be better, I told myself, than a good second-hand Bentley. There was an old three litre already in Colombo belonging to a friend called Bobby Shattock and I drove it once or twice and loved it. Shattock, poor chap, was killed in the RAF during the war. To resume, I wrote to an official in the Bentley Drivers' Club in England, a Colonel Berthon, told him what I wanted and asked for his advice. He was most helpful and he said there were two very good cars he would like me to see – one was a

163

three litre and the other a four and a half litre. Both were of early 1930 origin and he said they were mechanically sound but needed a little cosmetic work done on the open body work and upholstery. Colonel Berthon suggested I looked at them when I arrived, picked the one I wanted and he would then arrange for the necessary restoration work to be put in hand. When all was in order he would ship the car out to me in Colombo if my leave was over by that time. I was terribly excited by all this, agreed to all the good colonel's suggestions and started counting the days to when I sailed for England.

I was booked to sail in the Orient liner *Orsova*, leaving Colombo early in December 1957. I remember we were due to sail on a Monday because my friends gave me a marvellous farewell party at the Galle Face Hotel on the Saturday evening and I spent the Sunday recovering. It was pouring with rain on the Sunday and, donning an old pair of khaki shorts and a golf shirt I went for a long walk in the evening, in the monsoon rain, to try and get rid of my hangover. I pictured the *Orsova* heading towards Ceylon, she was about twelve hours steaming away. I realised I was forty-five (I felt 145 that evening), that I was still a bachelor and I wondered if there was some nice girl on the *Orsova* who would take pity on a rapidly becoming dissolute Colombo Wallah. There was.

10

1958 – 1963
Moose, Early Days in Colombo;
Advent of Julian and Andrew

Appu, my head boy, had packed for me on the Sunday and he
took my luggage on board at about lunch time on the Monday.
He used the office launch, met my steward on the *Orsova*,
unpacked and departed. As was usual in Leechman's, I
worked till the evening and then went on board myself, still in
office clothes. After a shower and a change into a more
respectable suit I met Stanley Williamson from the Chartered
Bank in Colombo who was also going home on leave. He was a
grass-widower and we had arranged to share a table for two in
the dining saloon for the voyage home. After a drink or two we
went down for our second-sitting dinner and then up on deck
to watch the ship slip her moorings and sail for Aden, a
wonderful moment for which I had waited for over two years.

The first morning at sea I was writing a few 'thank you'
letters when I saw a very attractive girl strolling around with
another girl. I saw her again at lunch, and at dinner, and I said
to Stanley Williamson, 'She looks nice.' 'Why don't you go
and talk to her?' said he. 'My dear chap,' I said, 'We haven't
been introduced and, anyway, we haven't reached Aden yet.'
We had a golden rule in those days that one kept to one's
Ceylon friends on board for the first few days and spoke to no
strangers. From bitter experience we had found that if one got
carried away and spoke to all and sundry on the first day or
two they were usually the wrong sort and one found it hard to

disentangle oneself. Matters came to a head as we were leaving
Aden – Stanley Williamson had Ann pinned to the rail and was
busily chatting her up. I joined them in nought seconds flat
and was introduced. It so happened that I had a curry lunch
party arranged in the ship's restaurant for the following day
and Ann accepted my invitation for herself and her friend to
join us. Ann's 'friend' in fact was her cousin, Patricia Hill, who
had been having a holiday in Australia with Ann and her
parents at their 'up-country' property in New South Wales.
We still see a good deal of Patricia and we regard her as one of
the family and we are very fond of her. We were then a
foursome and Ann and her cousin and Stanley and I did a lot
together for the rest of the voyage.

I found myself becoming fonder and fonder of Ann (Moose)
and watched her at deck games, Scottish dancing, etc, etc and
could find no fault. Perhaps the only fly in the ointment was
the glaring fact that I was much older than she and I felt the
discrepancy might be too much. So I set myself a limit of
twenty years – if Ann was twenty or more years younger than
me, that would be it, and I would say goodbye to her when we
reached Tilbury. One evening we were walking along the boat
deck after dinner, Ann in a flowing evening gown and me in a
black tie, when I slipped my arm through hers and said, 'How
old are you ducky?' She looked a bit boot-faced and asked why
I wanted to know. 'You'll find out soon enough,' I said, 'How
old are you?' 'Twenty-seven,' she said. That was an eighteen
year discrepancy, inside my limit (just!) and so I said, 'Good.'
'Why good?' she persisted. 'Patience dear, patience,' I said.
'All will become clear in due course.'

As you can imagine, I now had much food for thought. I
intended to propose but not whilst we were still on board – I
had heard too much about ship-board romances to fall for that
one. Then I considered my finances – these were satisfactory
but I felt I couldn't afford Ann *and* my Bentley and so, with
some sadness, I wrote to Colonel Berthon and explained the
position. I had a furnished house in Colombo and provided a)
Ann would be prepared to live out East and b) she was
prepared to put up with me, I could see my bachelor days

coming to a smart end.

Needless to say, we had a very happy voyage with some amusing trips ashore at Port Said, Naples and Marseilles. The evening before we docked at Naples there was a sweepstake on board and only sixty tickets were available at, I think, £5 a time, perhaps less. Anyway, the ship was due to pass under some overhead cables in the Straits of Messina and the sweep was won by the holder of the ticket giving the minute the ship's bridge cleared the cable. On returning to my cabin, after being ashore, there was a note from the purser on my dressing-table saying I had won. That took care of my bar bills for the rest of the voyage.

Moose threw a party in her cabin a night or so before we reached Tilbury and I acted as her barman, not difficult because her bath was full of bottles of champagne covered in ice and a good time was had by all.

On reaching Tilbury I offered to see Ann through passports and customs. Under 'Occupation' on her passport was 'Grazier.' I thought to myself 'that'll have to go.'

Moose was booked in at the International Sportsman's Club in Upper Grosvenor Street and I in the Lansdowne Club in Berkeley Square and so it could not have been a handier arrangement. As it was late December she departed promptly to Edinburgh to her relations for Christmas and I spent Christmas in London. My aunts who had looked after me as a small boy were still going strong and I spent Christmas Day with them. On Christmas morning a card was waiting for me at the Lansdowne and I had a feeling that if it was just a card then that would be that and, quite understandably, the cold Scottish air had dampened Ann's ardour. I kept that dreaded card, unopened, in my pocket until I had almost reached my aunts' house. I then drew the MG into the side of the road and opened the envelope. It was a very, *very* good card and it seemed my grazier friend would not be averse to seeing me again in the New Year.

Early in January I was summoned to Norfolk for lunch by the directors of the Norwich Union Life Insurance Society. Lunch was a splendid affair in the head office dining-room and the table was a sight with all the old society's silver on display and early spring daffodils everywhere. All the Life and Fire Society directors were there and I was a little uneasy because I had to be in London, at King's Cross Station, to meet Ann from Scotland at 8 pm. As coffee and brandy was being served the chairman, Sir Robert Bignold, got to his feet and said, 'Gentleman, I don't think we should detain Mr Bayne any longer – I believe he has a train to meet in London at 8 o'clock.' How the old devil knew I never found out but I had my suspicions.

I duly met Ann at King's Cross and on the way to her club I asked her what her plans were. 'I think I'm going to the Continent,' she said. 'No you're not,' I said and marvelled at my bravery. Well, we saw a lot of each other, did a number of shows, dined out and drove around in the MG.

One day a friend from Ceylon rang me at the Lansdowne and said could she possibly bring her daughters round for a swim in the club pool. Her name was Joan Hamilton and she had three young daughters – one of whom was Susannah York the actress. I invited them to lunch and quickly phoned Ann and asked her to come to my rescue. Well, the three young girls were full of beans, ate a huge lunch with much noise and seemed reluctant to go. I finally got them all away in a taxi and Ann said she really must go too – I told her sharply (my nerves were a little frayed by this time) that she would do no such thing as I wanted to talk to her in my room. 'It's against the Lansdowne rules,' she said but I would have none of it and dragged her off to Room 101. I closed the door and said, 'I've had it – Ann darling, will you please marry me?' 'I'd love to,' she said.

Ann phoned her parents in Australia and told them the news. They were not amused and who would blame them? Here was their little ewe lamb aged twenty-seven engaged to a completely unknown character of forty-five whom she had met on a boat and only known for a matter of five weeks. So disturbed were they that they made arrangements at once to fly to England to see what was going on. However, the day after we were engaged Ann took me to lunch in Hampstead to meet some cousins of hers. They were Sir Colin and Lady Anderson and they lived in Admirals House, a most lovely place. By a strange coincidence Sir Colin (Chairman of the Orient Line) announced the engagement of his own daughter, Catriona, at lunch that morning and so it was all pretty festive. What I didn't know was that the Andersons cabled Ann's parents as soon as we left to say that they had met me and there was no real need for them to worry as Ann could have done worse but not by much! Catriona was a bridesmaid at our wedding in June.

We then turned our attention to the matter of a ring. Moose said she would like an emerald and so, once again, I telephoned my dear Aimée de Saram in Colombo and asked for help. I said I wanted a large emerald with diamonds and she needn't worry too much about the price. Aimée did wonders, as usual, and sent the ring to England with a friend, by sea, and she handed it to Ann at tea in a hotel in London. I didn't see the bauble myself until I came back in June to marry Moose because my leave had expired and I had already sailed back to Colombo.

For the rest of my leave Ann and I travelled around meeting friends and relations and finally Ann took me up to Scotland to be 'inspected'. Moose has scores of relations over the border because her mother was a Scot. We were lavishly entertained during the inspection period and at the end we caught the night mail back to London. We couldn't get sleepers and so we sat up all night. The next morning we were strolling in Hyde Park and we sat down by the edge of the Serpentine. Ann was unusually quiet and I asked her what was wrong. 'Nothing,' she said. 'You've had it – haven't you?' I asked. She nodded and I said I was not too sure myself. So, terribly sadly, we were, of course, totally exhausted and drained, we decided to call the whole thing off. I told Ann I'd put her in a taxi but she said she would rather walk back to her club. I got back to the Lansdowne at noon, went to bed and didn't move until seven the next morning. I was shaving, after nineteen hours of solid sleep, and couldn't believe our engagement was off. I wiped the soap from my face and rang Ann. 'What are you doing?' I asked. 'I'm crying,' she said. I told her that I must have been mad yesterday and could we meet for a chat. She said her parents had arrived and she didn't know how she really felt. Anyway, we met, everything was 'on' again and I was to be 'on parade' for a final inspection by her parents at 7 pm at Grosvenor House that evening.

I duly appeared and found Mr and Mrs Cropper quite charming. I explained that I loved Ann and wanted to marry her – I added that I had never been married before, that I was a Christian, that I had never been to gaol, that I was a partner in my firm and could afford to keep Ann in reasonable comfort. This went down well and I think they felt perhaps I was not quite such a stinker as I might have been. Anyway, Mrs Cropper said that all seemed very satisfactory and added, 'And, of course, Ann has her own little nest egg.' I said that was nice to know but she wouldn't be needing it as I had enough to keep us happy. We all had dinner at Grosvenor House, Ann and I danced and I walked home greatly relieved that the trauma of the previous forty-eight hours was behind us. I never gave Ann's 'nest egg' another thought until about a week later when we were driving down to Sussex to have the MG serviced by a man I knew in Haywards Heath. 'What's this nest egg lark your Mum spoke about?' I asked. Ann told me. I pulled into the side of the road, stopped the car, and said, 'Say that again.' She did. 'That's far more than I've got,' I said. 'Yes,' she said!!

My leave ended in March 1958 and our plan was that we would marry in London in June. Ann's parents decided they would stay on in England until the great day and they rented a very nice flat in Berkeley Square and Ann moved in with them. I sailed back to Colombo on the P&O *Himalaya* and Ann saw me off at Tilbury. Jessie Matthews, the song and dance actress, was on board and she and I had more than one long talk on stage matters.

Ann and I were to be married 7 June at St Mark's Church in North Audley Street and, having put my affairs in order in Colombo I flew back to London about 4 June and had a nasty shock at Heathrow. I had Ann's wedding present, a pair of emerald and diamond earrings, burning a hole in my jacket pocket and proceeded towards Passport and Immigration.

170

Two officials were behind the Passport desk and I presented my passport. One gent opened it, looked at me, turned to the other man and said, 'This is the one you want, Joe.' I nearly died on the spot. The man said, 'We've had a signal from the Ceylon Police, sir, to say that your fiancée is outside and she probably doesn't want to be kept waiting – so we'll skip Customs and Immigration – please follow me.' I thanked him very much and said, 'I'm most grateful but please tell your colleague not to say 'This is the one you want Joe' in future!' Stanley de Saram, bless his old heart, was behind all this and he obviously had much influence in high places in Colombo.

Ann was staying with her parents at their flat in Berkeley Square and the wedding presents started arriving. People were very generous and we were given some lovely things. One present still stands out in Moose's mind – not so much the present itself, which was beautiful, but the manner in which it was delivered. There was a knock at the door and Ann opened it. Two men from Aspreys were standing there in full morning kit, you know, black tail coats, sponge-bag trousers – the lot. Each was carrying a large butler's tray and on them was a full set of Waterford crystal glasses for twelve people. Ann said it was a magnificent sight.

My best man was Alan Webber, younger brother of my wartime adjutant and at that time he was financial editor of *The News Chronicle Star.* We had the usual wedding rehearsal and on the Friday Alan took me out for my last bachelor night. This was a quite quiet affair and I was in bed in good time and in good order. On our wedding day Ann's father very kindly put a suite at Grosvenor House at the disposal of Alan and me and, having dropped a red rose outside the door of Ann's flat, I hurried into residence. Alan joined me and we had a drink or two whilst we were changing. We had another drink or two before lunch and, just as I was beginning to feel pretty good, my dear best man turned to me and said, 'You're really brave – I wouldn't go through this for a million pounds!' Charming!

Ann was only a little late and we were duly spliced. She looked enchanting even though she had lost a lot of weight which I believe a lot of brides do. The reception was at

171

Grosvenor House and it was a marvellous party with about 200 guests. After Ann had changed we left for The Savoy where I had booked a suite. Alan Webber called round with the telegrams and after a glass of champagne Ann and I were left in peace and we had a quiet dinner in our room. The next morning we left for Rome where we had a week at The Hasler, at the top of the Spanish steps. I had a nasty fright on our first evening – we had been for a walk and on our return I asked the concierge for our keys. 'Signor,' he said, 'A lady wishes to speak to you.' 'Some mistake,' I said feeling most alarmed. 'I'll get in touch with her later.' 'Signor,' said the man, 'she is waiting over there.' Ann's foot was tapping – she looked decidedly steely and I thought here ends our honeymoon. We looked where the concierge was pointing and three people got to their feet – two women and a man. I'd never seen any of them in my life before – they were *Ann's* friends. I was so relieved I asked them to dinner that evening and Ann was livid. 'What on earth did you do that for?' she demanded peevishly. 'Who told them we were living at The Hasler?' I asked.

After a blissful week we left for Colombo and arrived at Katunayake Airport, just after midnight, in the pouring rain with an emergency on and soldiers everywhere. On approaching Colombo our car was stopped several times with sodden soldiers shoving their guns inside the car and demanding to know who we were. Poor Ann, what an introduction to Serendib and she must have had thoughts on Bishop Heber's lines on Ceylon: 'Though every prospect pleases and only man is vile.'

We reached Shalimar – my bungalow – at about 2 am and it was a blaze of light with the servants immaculate in their white coats and sarongs ready to greet us on the front steps. The drive was flooded and so, in the proper manner, I carried my bride into the house. This looked like a small edition of the Chelsea Flower Show with all the flowers friends had sent Ann.

Ann soon settled down although it couldn't have been particularly easy for her because she knew no one and all our friends were, in fact, my friends. Anyway, she coped wonder-

172

fully well with her new life, despite the heat and humidity, and I was greatly relieved when I saw how quickly she adopted our sometimes strange and unfamiliar customs. The servants adored her although Appu, my head boy, played a trick on her early on. He never tried it on again.

Appu had been with me a long time, in fact I inherited him from my father and so he was allowed a degree of latitude that the other servants were not. Whilst I was a bachelor Appu would come to me every morning after breakfast with the 'cook's book'. It showed what he had bought the day before and how much it had all cost. We then agreed on the day's meals and I would give him more money. After Ann had been in Shalimar a month or so she said she would like to take over the cook's book and deal with Appu every morning. On the first morning, I had left for the office and Ann summoned Appu. 'Appu,' she said, 'I want to give master his favourite dinner this evening – what shall we have?' I knew nothing of this and we sat down to table at 8 pm as usual. We started with a clear soup in which floated bits of grease and raw carrot – this was followed by shepherd's pie and cabbage and instead of pudding we had a savoury – angels on horseback – prunes wrapped in bacon. Everything I detested, and Appu was under strict instructions never to produce them on pain of instant dismissal. Not wanting to hurt Ann's feelings, I soldiered through that disgusting meal with as good grace as I could muster and I thought Appu and the second servant were smirking a bit during the meal. After dinner I went into the kitchen and demanded an explanation. 'Good joke, master – no?' said Appu. I gave him hell but I couldn't really keep it up for long – the old devil. Ann was most relieved that those were, in fact, my most hated dishes and I think she forgave Appu with much relief the next morning.

Pretty soon after we were married Ann discovered that Julian was on the way and although the first few months were not too bad for her I could see she was finding everything a bit of a strain. So we decided it would be best for Ann to go to her parents in Australia and have Julian there.

I should have said earlier that Ann's hobby was breeding

poodles and she did this with some success on her parents' property Greenhills, some 250 miles north of Sydney. Ann's favourite was the mother of her litters – Judy – and she was a black miniature and clearly a champion in every way. Ann sent for her and she arrived in a crate from Sydney in which Ann's sister Joan had thoughtfully put a pair of old red corduroy slacks of Ann's to keep Judy happy and for her to know (and she undoubtedly did) that Ann would be waiting at the end of the journey. We collected Judy at the airport and, once out of her crate, she first spent a penny in a discreet and most ladylike way, and then gave Ann the most wonderful welcome. I was totally ignored by poodle and owner but they were both ecstatically happy and so who was I to object! Once home Judy settled down and Ann made her go through her considerable repertoire of tricks. For instance, she would beg and balance a chocolate on the end of her nose until allowed to eat it. She could walk the length of a room on her hind legs and, with her 'show poodle' cut looked enchanting I must admit. But that damn dog was as cold as ice towards me and it was only her good manners that prompted her to acknowledge me now and again.

Well, the time came for Ann to leave for Australia and I felt very sad driving her to the airport. We said our goodbyes and I drove home wondering how the devil I had stayed a bachelor for so long. It was evening when I got home and I had my bath and settled down to have a few drinks to cheer me up before ordering dinner. Judy was lying on a rug staring at me when suddenly she came up to me and, with no encouragement from me, started doing some of her tricks. I have never under-estimated a dog's intelligence since that evening – she knew I was sad, and she was too, and so she decided to cheer me up. We became the greatest friends.

I've just remembered something that happened before Ann left for Australia. As I said earlier, the heat in Colombo was getting her down and the early stages of her pregnancy didn't help either. So it was arranged that Ann would spend a week or so with our great friends Roy and Sheila Webber on their tea estate, Fordyce, in the Dikoya district about 4,500 feet up. I

174

drove Ann up, spent the night with the Webbers and drove back to Colombo promising to pick Ann up at the end of her stay. Roy Webber, if you remember, was my adjutant during the war and we were great friends. It so happened that Moose's birthday fell on the Saturday before she was due to return to Colombo and she knew that I would be arriving on the Saturday morning some time. What she didn't know was that I left Colombo at the God-forsaken hour of 3 am, in the dark, and reached Fordyce at about 6.30 am. Some of the servants were moving around but they knew me well and didn't let on that I had arrived. I should explain that the Fordyce bungalow was almost entirely surrounded by wide verandahs and so it followed that every bedroom opened out on to a verandah. I knew, of course, where Ann's room was and sneaked along the verandah to her open door without making a sound. I walked into the room and there was Ann, asleep as I thought, under a vast pink mosquito net. She must have heard me because she rolled over and said in a voice dripping with coyness 'Is that you, Roy?' I said, 'No! it bloody well isn't Roy – it's me!' I very nearly didn't give her her birthday present which was an emerald and diamond eternity ring. Everyone at breakfast had hysterics when I told them the story.

As May 1959 approached I anxiously waited for news about my first offspring. I had a friend who carried some muscle with the central telegraph office in Colombo and he had arranged for me to be informed by telephone as soon as a cable from Australia arrived. Of course, Appu and the others knew where I was at all times and, in fact, I was at a cocktail party given by Aimée and Stanley de Saram when Appu phoned through and he read out the cable to me. It said, 'Julian arrived safely early this morning and we are both well. Looks just like you darling – love – Ann.' I read this out to the party and you can imagine the reaction! Someone said, 'Don't worry, dear boy – he'll grow out of it.' Another said, 'Perhaps some zoo will take him in.' I had a lot of friends.

I engaged the services of a nanny whilst Ann was away and so she was ready for duty when Ann and Julian returned home.

It was a great day and it was a wonderful moment at Katunayake Airport when I greeted Ann, carrying Julian, and I caught my first glimpse of my son. I was a little puzzled by his red hair as there was no history of this in either Ann's family or mine but after some reflection I gave her the benefit of the doubt.

We all seemed to fit into Shalimar quite snugly but a year or so later, when Andrew was on the way, we realised we would have to find a larger house. Ann was quite happy to have Andy in Colombo and we had an excellent Tamil lady doctor and a first-class British nursing home. I remember Andrew's arrival all too well. The first signs started just after dinner and I rushed Ann off to the Frazer Home. She was admitted and I was sent back to the car to await events. The doctor didn't arrive until after midnight and, when she did appear, she rushed across the lawn with her sari flying. So far so good but then nothing seemed to happen until about 5 am when people started dashing from the maternity ward across to the main hospital and rushing back with oxygen cylinders and all manner of sinister things. I was having fits watching all this but I was under strict instructions from the doctor that I was to go nowhere near Ann until she told me I could. I had lost all hope of having another son, or a daughter, and I was quite sure something dreadful had happened. It was just after dawn when a large Asian gentleman emerged from the operating theatre on to the lawn. He was covered in blood from head to foot and I knew my worst fears were about to be realised. I went up to him and said I was the father. He looked me up and down and said, 'Oh – good show – congratulations – you have a fine son!' I almost wept with relief.

Instead, I drove home to bath and change and met Stanley de Saram on the way having his early morning walk and I gave him the good news. I had seen nothing of the doctor by this time and so I had no idea of how bad a time Ann had had, but I feared the worst with all that blood on the man I had spoken to. I had some breakfast and returned to the nursing home. I crept into Ann's room in case she was asleep – not a bit of it – she was sitting up in bed looking as bright as a button and tucking into scrambled eggs! Andrew was indeed a fine son. I had a sapphire and diamond ring for Ann in my pocket as a small reward.

We found a nice house in the Cinnamon Gardens area of Colombo and the four of us settled in there very comfortably. It was a flat-roofed concrete bungalow and therefore very hot – it also leaked like the very devil when it rained. Ann had our bedroom and the boys' nursery air-conditioned, which was a great comfort to us all. The house was called Lomond and we had some happy years there until we finally left Ceylon for good in 1963. A very sad thing happened – one evening Ann and I had come home from a dinner party and, as usual, we let Judy, the poodle, out for a little walk down the drive to spend a penny. There was a wretched cat in the road – Judy saw it and dashed after it and a lunatic in a passing car killed her outright. It was awful for us all.

One day, just before we moved to Lomond and we were still at Shalimar, I was at a Chamber of Commerce meeting – I represented the insurance interests in the island. The telephone rang and the secretary picked up the receiver, paused for a moment and passed it to the Chairman. He listened and said, 'What? – What? Are you sure? Please keep me posted.' He turned to us and said, 'Gentlemen – there is a rumour that the prime minister has been assassinated.' I said, 'If you'll pass me the phone I'll see if it is a rumour or not.' He did and I rang Moose at our bungalow. We lived about three or four hundred yards from Mr Bandaranike's house, Taprobane. I asked Ann to look towards Taprobane but not, in any circumstances, to go into the road – I said I'd hold the line. She came back and said there were ambulances, police cars and blue lights flashing everywhere. I told our chairman he could take it that an attempt had been made to assassinate the prime minister. The full story came out later, of course, but I was afraid that if the assassin was a Christian, Hindu or Muslim we were all in for a tricky time – in fact the assassin was a genuine Buddhist priest. The prime minister was a small, frail man although not very old – in his fifties I would say – but his stamina and resistance were remarkable as you will see. The assassin had armed himself with a .45 army revolver, a weapon that throws a very heavy lead slug which enters the body quite neatly, does a horrifying amount of damage inside and then, sometimes, leaves through a hole the size of a saucer – not nice. The Buddhist priest had armed himself with this army forty-five revolver and had loaded all six chambers. He had called at Taprobane and asked to see the PM personally. Mr Bandaranike, not wanting to offend a Buddhist priest, walked on to the verandah where the monk was waiting with the revolver concealed in his yellow robes. On the PM approaching him, the priest drew the revolver, cocked it, and fired point-blank, hitting Mr Bandaranike in the chest. The PM turned and ran into the house with the priest following and firing. All six bullets were fired and the PM was hit five times. He lived for some eighteen hours, I believe, and it was little short of a miracle that any man could survive for even a few minutes with five large .45 slugs inside him. The priest was tried, found guilty and hanged and the PM's widow succeeded him as prime minister of Sri Lanka.

Early in 1962 one or two clouds started to appear on the horizon and these were unsettling. The first matter of moment was that a much larger firm than Leechman & Co. made an offer for us that two of the partners felt they couldn't refuse and so we were taken over by, let us call them, Cardomom Ltd. Cardomom did the same sort of business that Leechman's did but on a much larger scale. Bartlett and I were not particularly happy at the take-over and we were even less happy when I happened to overhear an 'unofficial' arrangement that would, if implemented, have had a disastrous effect on Bartlett's and my shares. This deal was not in any way instigated by Cardomom's but it would have made them very happy had it gone through. Well, I stepped in and said I was no longer ready to go through with the merger and they could count me out. I had my way and the 'arrangement' was dropped but I was not popular. Whilst I was still smarting at the injustice of things I was asked by our high commissioner to go and see him. This I did and he said that one of the characters in the merger was in line for a C.B.E. and would I please do the citation.

What our high commissioner did not know (and I did) was that this gentleman was on the verge of throwing in his hat and leaving Ceylon. I was sure that the C.B.E. would not be forthcoming if the facts were known and, as I've said, I was pretty cross with some people at the time. However, I decided not to be bitchy, although I had ample reason to be, and did the citation and the C.B.E. was duly awarded.

Then Mrs Bandaranaike, the PM, decided to nationalize all insurance in the island. This added to my workload a lot and I found myself representing the Life Offices in London, the Fire Offices Committee in London and, at the same time, trying to protect the interests of all the British insurance agents in Colombo. As if this was not enough, the Commissioner for Insurance, appointed by Mrs Bandaranaike, was new to the business and he used to consult me regularly as to what he should do. He even used to call on me at my bungalow at dead of night, for consultations, with a blanket over his head in case he was recognised by someone! Anyway, I didn't really mind because he was grateful and helped my cause with considerable co-operation. I had more than one meeting with the Minister of Industries but all to little avail and nationalization went through.

Now we go back to Ann's 'little nest egg' which her mother mentioned when we first met if you remember. In 1962 there was no reciprocal tax agreement between the UK and Ceylon and so Ann's UK and other investments were lumped together with my income and so we were paying over 100% in tax. You see, Moose was paying UK tax plus Ceylon tax on her world income and there was no relief for paying double tax. A situation which obviously could not be allowed to continue. Add to this that Ceylon Exchange Control was becoming harsher and harsher and so I was worried out of my wits as to what to do. Don't forget I was now working for a strange (sic) firm too and you will see I was not wildly happy.

However, leave was due and the four of us sailed away in May 1963 in the *Iberia* for England.

11

1963 and Sarah and Beyond

Before leaving for our holiday a friend suggested we look at houses whilst on leave. He said, 'You'll look at fifty, hate the lot but at least it will be good experience for you both against the time when you will have to buy a house in England – a time which can't be far off.' We had rented a small house in Kent, not far from Tunbridge Wells, and it was quite the coldest little dwelling we had ever known. We put our names down with one or two estate agents and the brochures came flooding in. We wondered if indeed we would see fifty houses and 'hate the lot'. We saw two, which we hated, and the third one we fell for hook, line and sinker. It belonged to Lord Denning – the Master of the Rolls – and we were invited to tea. Ann's Aunt Violet was spending a few days with us at the time and so we took her along too. The house and garden were lovely and they were in Cuckfield in Sussex and we were very excited until I asked the price. Lord Denning told me and our excitement evaporated on the spot. I tried to haggle a bit but to no avail, so we thanked the Dennings for their hospitality and departed. We were very disappointed but the price, for 1963, was, I thought, enormous and so I said to Moose, 'It's one of those things and kindly oblige me by not mentioning the matter again.' We took Aunt Vi to dinner in Brighton, not a word about the house was said, and finally we drove sadly back to our little igloo in Kent.

The next morning we left Julian and Andrew with Nanny and got into the car to go shopping. I was just going to start the engine when Moose turned to me and said, 'What about that house?' I said, 'We've got to have it – haven't we?' She said, 'Of course!' So we sat in the car and altered the whole course of our lives. We decided that Ann, Nanny and the boys would stay in England, I would resign from Cardomom's but would go back to Colombo for twelve months to wind up our affairs, try and get the nationalization of insurance under control and try and not let Cardomom's down with too great a bump. My letter of resignation was not well received.

Moose and I then went back to the Dennings and, having got nowhere on a price reduction, I explained we had to be in residence by such and such a date, if we were to buy Fairclose, because I had to sail back to Colombo. Lord Denning turned to his wife – 'Joan, darling,' he said, 'I don't think Mr Bayne realises I am Master of the Rolls – obviously he has never heard of John Profumo, Christine Keeler or Mandy Rice-Davies.' He said it very nicely and I assured him I was very much aware of the John Profumo scandal and that I also knew he was conducting the enquiry. The Dennings were marvellous, they moved out and we moved in in sufficient time for me to catch the *Himalaya* back to Colombo.

So far so good, but I was a little worried at leaving Moose alone with Nanny and the two little boys for such a long time. However, just before I sailed Ann's mother wrote from Sydney to say she was coming to England and would like to spend some time at Fairclose. She had been invited by the family firm to launch a new ship in Sweden and Moose had been invited too – I found this to be very good news indeed. All went according to plan and Ann had her mother for company for some time.

I duly arrived back in Colombo to work out my year's notice and the atmosphere was frosty to say the least and I regretted having been so generous in giving twelve months' notice. However, I had a lot on my plate and the time went very quickly indeed. At the office I was busy with the nationalization of insurance business, resigning from various directorships, giving up committees and generally offloading my responsibilities which had accumulated over a number of years.

On the domestic front, I agreed with Moose as to what she

wanted shipped back to England from our house Lomond and what was to be sold in Colombo by auction. We had some nice Dutch things which were very old, a chest and a cabinet, and these were classed as 'antiques' and the Ceylon Customs would not allow them out of the island. Well, I ordered two lift vans to take all the things we were allowed to ship and these were parked in our drive with the loading and packing people in attendance and we waited for the customs' men to arrive. They showed up eventually and I took them round the house to show them everything that was going to be shipped. I had the wireless on at the time as I was listening to an England and Australia test match being played at Lords. One Customs man stopped to listen and said, 'Sir, is that the test match?' I said it was. 'Can we listen?' he asked. 'Of course,' I said. 'Would you like a beer whilst you're listening?' 'Oh, sir, yes please,' they said. 'What about all these things?' I asked pointing to our Dutch chest and cabinet. 'Pack everything,' they said, 'also the brown box and the brown cupboard.' So we got our antiques home.

Everything that was left at Lomond I sold at an auction held in the house. I then moved into the Galle Face Hotel intending to spend the rest of my 'year's notice' there. I had a lovely room overlooking the sea and the swimming pool and I was most comfortable. This state of affairs didn't last long however because Reggie Bois, who lived alone in the vast George Stewart house, invited me to stay in the annexe for the remainder of my time in the island. This I did until that wonderful day when Ann, Julian and Andrew came out to collect me eventually to take me home, via Australia and Singapore, after thirty four years' service in Ceylon.

Reggie and Bene Bois (she was the one who had the crabs that were 'tired after the bicycle ride') were great friends of ours and we saw a lot of each other when we were all back in England. Bene sadly died in the early 1980s and Reggie continued to come and visit us regularly in Sussex. About 1983 Reggie stopped coming so Ann rang him up to ask what was wrong. He said, 'I've only got a few weeks to live Ann – I've got cancer.' Ann terribly shocked, left the matter for a month and rang again. 'It's tomorrow, Ann,' said Reggie, 'I am due to die tomorrow.' He did.

Before I left Ceylon, a year or two before, two good friends of mine, Antony Riley and Neil Pearce came to see me. Neil said that an old friend of his father's was about to retire in London and wanted to sell his insurance broking business in Westminster and was Neil interested? Neither Antony nor Neil knew a great deal about insurance but they were on the verge of leaving Ceylon and they wondered if they should look more deeply into the offer. I asked them to send for the accounts for the previous three years and when I had seen these I'd let them know what I thought. The accounts were not exactly brilliant but I felt with some hard work, Tony and Neil could make a go of it. After all, jobs for men over fifty-five were not easy to come by in the 1960s. They took my advice, thoroughly enjoyed themselves and in 1965, soon after we had all returned to England, invited me to join them. This I did and spent fifteen years in the partnership.

Ann, the boys and I, arrived back in England towards the end of 1964 and, soon after this, Ann started to feel a bit sick in the mornings – Sarah was on the way. There was to be some drama, however, before my darling daughter arrived. Ann had been out shopping one morning and, having deposited her parcels in the kitchen at Fairclose, was making her way, at high speed, towards the dining-room with a bag of plums in her hand. On turning a corner a runner on the polished parquet floor slipped under her feet and she fell, trapping her right leg against our oak chest in the hall. We both heard the leg break. Poor Ann, it was the most awful shock. A telephone was on the oak chest just above where Ann was lying and I dialled 999 and an ambulance carted Ann and me away in a very short time. Ann's doctor, a character called 'Cocky' Farr said that was the end of Ann's pregnancy and there was no hope whatever of the baby surviving the shock of the broken leg. Well, Ann's pregnancy progressed, 'Cocky' Farr kept on, parrot-like, repeating, 'There'll be no baby, you know,' and Moose engaged the services of a wonderful physiotherapist from Haywards Heath to massage her leg. When the news of the broken leg reached Ceylon, Aimée de Saram at once air-mailed a bottle of the most evil-smelling liquid to Ann. This was a mixture of bear oil and peacock oil prepared by an Ayurvedic monk in Colombo. When Ann's physio arrived that evening I somewhat shame-facedly produced the bottle – 'Don't laugh,' I said and told him how it had arrived and what was in it. 'Mr Bayne,' he said, 'I never mock at anything from an ayurvedic source – let's have it.' It was marvellous and the physio said he'd never seen such a quick recovery.

I teased 'Cocky' Farr quite a lot during the following few months about his pessimism over the pregnancy and then one night, after dinner, Ann started having pains – I shot her round to hospital and she went straight into the labour room. I was waiting outside in the corridor when 'Cocky' Farr came flying up the stairs at the double doing up his white coat. I called out, 'What about the baby now?' He yelled back, 'Oh, shut up!!' Some thirty minutes later a nurse brought in a small bright red object, held upside down by its feet. 'Your daughter, sir,' she said. Moose had an easy time of it and we were overjoyed at having a daughter – in fact we reckoned we now had the perfect family and we would call it a day. Although there is a six year gap between Julian and Sarah their birthdays are only one and a quarter hours away from each other 5 May and 6 May.

We had to extend Fairclose when Sarah arrived and we built a flat for Nanny and Lewis, her husband, above our large double garage. Behind this we built on a playroom for the children. One day I noticed flames and smoke behind the brand new playroom. I dashed round fearing the worst and there was Andrew, aged about five, matches in hand looking proudly at a huge bonfire raging right against the new playroom wall. 'Who started that bonfire?' I roared. Andrew looked up at me, guilt written all over him. 'What bonfire, Daddy?' he asked.

By this time, May 1965, I had had a few months at my new job in Westminster with Neil Pearce and Tony Riley. I was horrified to find how small the firm was and the annual premium income was meagre in the extreme. I went to Pearce and Riley and told them that I honestly didn't think they could afford me. I mean dividing the profits two ways between Neil and Tony was bad enough but dividing them three ways to include me was ludicrous. I said I would like to enlarge the firm substantially but it would mean harder and more work all round, bigger staff, etc. We were only doing life assurance and annuities when I arrived and I opened up fire, accident and marine departments. Conditions improved and when I retired the firm was six times bigger than it had been.

During the years I was commuting to London two things happened at Haywards Heath Station. The first one was amusing and the second one quite interesting. The funny one happened one morning when I was standing in a queue waiting to renew my season ticket and in front of me was a mother with her little daughter aged, say, two in a child's harness. The little girl turned round to me and I made a funny face (an easy matter for me!) and she was giggling away when her mother turned round and looked at me rather sternly imagining, I suppose, that I was a child molester. To cover my embarrassment I smiled at the mother and said, 'Her first journey perhaps eh?' The mother replied rather frostily, 'In fact not, she has just been to Bahrain and back by Concorde.' I collapsed.

The other thing happened one morning when I was about to walk upstairs to my platform when Harold Macmillan, who was then our ex-prime minister, was about to travel to London with his grand-daughter. A vast suitcase stood between the two and they were arguing amicably about who should carry it upstairs. They both looked incapable – one too old and one too young – so I stepped between them and took the suitcase upstairs to the London platform. They were both most grateful and I asked where I should leave the suitcase. 'Just here,' said Mr Macmillan. 'You see my grand-daughter travels second-class but I go up to the front of the train.' Whilst we were walking there Mr Macmillan remarked to me that we needed more porters. I replied that what we really needed was the type called a 'rupee porter.' These were men, on most of the Indian stations, and they wore a sort of strawberry red shirt outside

185

their dhotis with 'Rupee Porter' in large letters across the front. These men could carry the most incredible amount of baggage with the aid of straps attached to their shoulders and waist. Mr Macmillan turned to me and he said, 'I know them well and have used them on many occasions.' He paused and added, 'You know – I am worried about India – they should be eating those cows not worshipping them!' I thought this was the most wonderfully intelligent remark but, then, he was a great man.

We had one or two other interesting and amusing incidents in the office. One, I remember, concerned an air-marshall. He had recently sued a publisher for libel and had been given 25,000 guineas in the court award. He was highly delighted and asked us to quote for an annuity costing 25,000 guineas. We asked him to call back in a few days' time to examine our quotations and sign a proposal form. Call back he did and as he sat down he said, 'Gentlemen, I'm sorry to be boring but could you please re-quote for twenty-five thousand *pounds* instead of twenty-five thousand guineas – you see, I've spent the 'guineas'. He was the most likeable and attractive man and when he was a young officer in the RAF, during the war, he must have broken a few hearts. Naturally we knew a lot about his affairs, because he was a very good client of ours, and it caused us some amusement some years later when we learnt that his will had provided for the bulk of his estate to go to his widow but his Bentley was to go to another lady who was also our client. Both ladies complained to us quite acidly.

Then I was involved in a case where a young tea planter, was, with his sister, about to inherit a large property from their father. To be precise, the father had already given the property to his two children and the estate duty laws at that time required that the father, the donor, survived for five years from the date of the gift if the value of the property was not to be added back to his estate. We advised the young planter and his sister to insure the father's life for five years for a sum equal to the value of the gifted property – over £150,000. This was because if the father unfortunately died within the five year *inter vivos* period, the property would be added back to his

186

estate for death duty purposes but if they took our advice, the children would get the value of the property under the life insurance policy. I called for quotations and one was far superior to the others. I queried the quotation because, to me, it seemed palpably wrong but the insurance company assured me it was correct. I rang them up again and told them their quotation was wrong. 'Not so,' they said, 'we have re-checked it and it is correct.' Before completing a proposal form I wrote to the insurance company and, once again, said their quotation was wildly incorrect. By this time Neil and Tony thought I had taken leave of my senses and told me to clinch the deal without any more fuss. I waited for the insurance company's written reply which once again said they stood by their quotation and so I had a proposal form completed by the young planter and his sister, on their father's life, and I sent this with the first year's premium to the insurance company. About eighteen months later the old father suddenly died. I slammed in a claim on the insurance company for £150,000 and, would you believe it, they wrote and said they couldn't pay because the premium was wrong! I went straight round to the general manager of the company, put the correspondence in front of him, told him that I had queried the quotation three times and added that my solicitor would love to hear about it. They paid.

At the time I joined the firm the main source of income was from the professors and other senior academics from the universities throughout the British Isles. These ladies and gentlemen retired each year on, I think, 30 September and they belonged to a superannuation fund known as the FSSU which, if I remember correctly, stands for the Federated Superannuation System for Universities. Anyway, about June or July each year we used to write to all the university bursars and tell them that, as usual, we would be happy to meet, help and advise any members retiring in September. We used to get an astonishing number of responses and from October to April, each year we used to be very busy trying to help these clients. Some cases were very sad and, although we did our best, we used to worry a lot as to how on earth some people were going to manage for the rest of their lives. I mean, all professors were simply brilliant in their particular fields but when it came to worldly knowledge such as buying a house, or buying a pound of potatoes from the greengrocers, they were utterly lost. One couple I remember well – they were husband and wife, in different colleges, and they both retired on the same day. They had lived in college, had the benefit of the college servants and other amenities and had hardly ever shopped for food or cooked it. They had about £80,000 between them and one or two small investments. We explained they would need to buy a house and once they had done this there would not be a lot left from the £80,000 on which they would have to live for the rest of their lives. They left our office totally bewildered and very worried. It was all very sad and it happened more than once.

Before I leave the matter of my partnership, you might find a thumb-nail sketch on my two colleagues to be educational. Riley first. He was a small man, about five foot six inches tall and dapper and smart beyond belief. He was the kindest man imaginable and the most exquisite snob, but in the nicest way. 'Davis makes my clothes Alan' he would say or 'Lobb makes my boots'. I asked him once, 'Aren't Lobbs very expensive?' He looked down his splendid 'Wellington' nose. 'You mean there's someone else I could go to?' Riley was a dear man and I was very fond of him and felt I had lost more than a friend when he died. He had married a most attractive American girl called Olive who came from the 'deep South', with the appealing accent that those 'southern folk' have.

Now we turn to Pearce. The exact opposite of Riley. A huge man with a voice to match his size. He was six foot two inches and about sixteen stone and he had been to Haileybury. Pearce had a wonderfully happy-go-lucky nature and was never happier than when Riley or I were doing all the work and he was stamping around the office making a great deal of noise: a very very likeable giant and one who loved his little tot at any time of the day or night. He said to me once, 'Alan, now that you live in England and have given up your bad Ceylon drinking habits, how much whisky do you drink?' I replied, 'Well, as you know, Ann doesn't drink whisky and, if my friends leave me alone, I can make a bottle last four or five

188

days.' 'I don't believe it,' said Pearce. 'Marjorie and I try and make three bottles last two days.' He had a stroke a few years later and, when he died after a few months' illness he weighed over twenty stone. Poor Neil, he was such a kind and generous man and I was very sad when he died. In fact, I often used to think how very lucky I was to have two such marvellous partners as Tony and Neil.

About this time my thoughts started turning towards the purchase of a suitable carriage because we only had a little Mini Traveller at the time belonging to Ann. I looked at a number of second-hand Bentleys and fell for a 1955 Mark VI for which I paid the princely sum of £450. A few years later, when I bought a Bentley SI, I only got £135 for the Mark VI as a trade-in. The family kept me busy, and have continued to do so, in the matter of buying and selling cars and houses. I've no idea as to the number of cars that have changed hands but I have been involved in twenty-two house or flat conveyances since 1963 and I hope to goodness we are now all happily settled, for the time being anyway.

While Sarah was at her prep school her headmistress came to me one day and said that she was a governor of a girls' public school in Buckinghamshire. She added that the school was in all sorts of difficulties and would I consider joining the governors as a sort of trouble-shooter. The idea appealed to me and I said I would but, alas, it was too late and the 'troubles' were too established for me to be able to do much good. For instance, I found the school was owed over £40,000, from defaulting parents, all the insurance policies had expired, one teacher only did one half-hour period a week, and goodness only knows what else. So after two years as a governor our accountants advised us to close down. It was such a shame because this school was housed in the most lovely buildings, steeped in history, and had great charm, but the damage was done.

The children have now grown up all too quickly and the family holidays we all used to love, from the very early ones at Studland Bay in Dorset, to the chartered cruiser trips on the Canal du Midi are things of the past. A little drama occurred whilst we were all on one of our chartered cabin cruiser trips on the Canal du Midi in the south of France. Sarah was about three, I suppose, and, one morning, she and the boys were playing on the tow-path near where we were moored. She had her beloved little monkey puppet on her hand. This was a dear little fellow with a red fez on his head. I was standing near the bows of the boat with Moose when the three started to come on board. Sarah came first, missed her footing and went straight into the canal and disappeared. I went in after her (watch and all!), and then the real horror began. I couldn't find Sarah. It was a beautiful sunny day and I could see quite clearly under water but there was no sign of my little sibling. I searched and searched. I could see the hull of the boat above me, but no Sarah. I cannot describe my feelings of desolate panic. I came up for air and there, thank heavens, was Sarah, on board, monkey puppet still on hand and safely in Ann's arms. I almost wept with relief. Ann told me later what had happened. As I hit the water Sarah bobbed up to the surface and was fished out by Moose. I think Ann and I finished off a bottle of gin before we cast off, so relieved were we that we were once again sailing with five Baynes, and not four.

It was on this trip, I think, that Julian and Andrew came rushing up to Moose one morning crying and in a great state and yelling they had worms and were about to die. They were about seven and nine years old. We hoved to, moored the boat and went to inspect our little darlings' stools. Moose didn't seem too worried about what she saw – I didn't look – but the little lads refused to be comforted. I had a brainwave, 'I know just the thing to cure these worms,' I said and gave them each a tin of ice-cold lager – the first they'd ever had. It did the trick, and our trouble then was to try and calm down two quite sozzled little mariners rushing happily all over the boat.

We also visited Ceylon and Sydney and these things too now belong to the past. A last little anecdote about my darling daughter: When Sarah was a baby we were having one of our winter holidays in Australia. We were living in a motel in Sydney and we were all there, including Nanny. One morning Moose had gone off to see her mother, and Nanny and I took

Sarah and the boys for a walk in the park at Rushcutters Bay. Nanny, resplendent in a saree, had Sarah in her pram and the boys and I had walked on ahead as they were busy looking for shells along a sandy strip near the bay. We must have been about 200 yards ahead of Nanny and Sarah when something made me look round. There was a man standing beside Sarah's pram and Nanny was looking very agitated and waving her arms about. I hared back (I could still run quite fast in those days!) and by this time Nanny had Sarah in her arms and was pushing the man away. I grabbed him round the neck and asked Nanny what was going on. 'This man says Sarah is his sister and he's going to take her away,' she said. 'I think not,' I said and told Nanny to take Sarah and the boys back to our motel and I would take care of the kidnapper. I let them get away and then I frog-marched my unshaven and smelly friend to the road. On the way I explained to him, in some detail, that I was going to hand him over to the police and that I was going to see to it, personally, that he went to gaol for about 400 years. He didn't seem to care for this idea and whinged away and pleaded to be let go and he would never do it again, etc, etc. The man was clearly a 'nut' and by the time we got to the park gates I was getting a bit bored by the whole thing and people were staring and he was getting smellier and smellier so I relented. I let him go and said I was going to watch him out of sight and if I ever saw him again I would get really cross. He went. I think the truth of the matter was I had no wish to get involved in a long-drawn-out police case and ruin our holiday. Wrong, I suppose.

The school days are over and, mercifully, so are the journeys Moose and I used to have to make to the schools for exeats. The horror one was when the boys at Harrow, and Sarah at Benenden had exeats on the same weekend. The schools were, I suppose, over 100 miles apart, in opposite directions and Moose would go one way and I the other. Still, it was, on looking back, the greatest fun.

Julian came to me one day, when he was twenty-five or so, and said, 'Dad, you must sometimes be rather disappointed in me.' I asked him why on earth that should be so. He said,

'Well, Andrew was head boy at Harrow and Sarah was head girl at Benenden and I've never been anything.' I took the unhappy and remorse-stricken lad aside. 'I seem to remember,' I said, 'I had a son once who won the Winston Churchill prize for English essay at Harrow and who then went on to win an open scholarship to Oxford – a son who was so brainy we still refer to him as 'The absent-minded professor.' 'Oh Dad,' said Julian, 'well, if you put it like that.'

Looking back over nearly eighty years I realize I've been very lucky for most of my life. There were, of course, some moments or periods in the early days I could have well done without – who couldn't? – but I've been blessed with a wonderful family who are a source of great happiness to me.

Soon after I had joined Leechmans a small Ceylonese gentleman called Gomez used to call on me every year to collect a subscription for his monthly journal called *The Searchlight*. This was an entertaining little magazine not unlike our *Private Eye* but perhaps a little gentler. I was always struck by a small text at the head of the first article in every issue. It read:

> *For the cause that needs assistance,*
> *For the wrongs that need resistance,*
> *For the future, in the distance,*
> *For the good that I may do.*

I was always moved by that little text and I used to try and live up to it. Well, anyway, I tried.

So this is the end of my reminiscing, I think, because you all know everything that has happened since. And, so, as someone once wrote:

> *My inkwell is dry,*
> *My pen's on the shelf*
> *If you want any more,*
> *You can write it yourself.*

12

'Odd Flood Ode'

I wrote these verses in Jaela, near Colombo and where I was encamped, whilst I was still smarting at the unjust treatment I had received from Base Area, the HQ of the Ceylon Defence Force.

You will have already read about the flooding of Usk Valley earlier in the book.

ODD FLOOD ODE

Here's a tale of rushing waters,
Tardy cries of 'shouldn't oughters',
Brass Hats getting clever after
Submersion of the topmost rafter.

Criticisms, howls of anger,
Vieing with the Peleng Ganga,
In its roaring, headlong torrent,
Screams of 'Pay stopped', 'Royal Warrant'.

But, 'tut, I rush upon my fences,
Let's marshall facts, eschew pretences
And, without more shilly shally
Record the flooding of Usk Valley.

It must have been in mid-September,
(The day and time I can't remember)
The martial limelight stopped to spy
Upon 'D' Coy, Fourth CLI.

'Why aren't these men in fitter fettle?
Why aren't they ready to give battle?'
'Because they're doing guards?' 'What rot!'
'How many? What? The bloody lot?'

Thus quoth Base Area and some more,
'You should have told us long before.
You did? There's nothing we can find
To prove – Arrh'm!! Well, never mind.'

'Now *we* will find a place for training
A land of sun, with little raining.
So get the map, don't dilly dally,
Why! here's the very spot – Usk Valley.'

194

'So make your camp upon the greens,
With soakage pits and trench latrines,
And every tent must have it's drain
To catch the little drops of rain.'
            (Oh! Goody, Goody)

I sent a party in advance
To pitch the camp and then perchance
To wait and watch for us, with smiles,
Who'd marched the thirty blood-stained miles.

With destination reached at dusk
We gazed upon this valley – Usk,
And by the light of parting day
I must admit it looked OK.

So then we bathed and ate and drank,
And on our backs to earth we sank,
For twelve hours' sleep to make us well,
We'd done our stuff – but what the hell!

The 'Lights Out' bugle was the call
For leeches big and leeches small,
To stagger forth with shambling gait
Upon our frames to masticate.

The leech is such a sordid beast
Who by a recce 'fore his feast
Eliminates the chance of heart-burn
By feeding just above the sunburn.

But later on the bugs and ticks,
Leeches, with their vulgar tricks,
Felt their nuisance value lower
Watching us out-Noah'ing Noah.

For just one week the elements
Kept us waiting in suspense,
Then Pluvius struck with all his powers,
On Sunday, twenty hundred hours.

'What heavy rain!' I said to me,
'It's sure to finish presently,'
And yet I felt uneasiness
When the downpour grew no less.

For four hours' full it rained like hell,
The river's breast began to swell.
It's voice became a sullen thunder
And so I called my Guard commander.

With this stout henchman by my side
In silence watched the leaping tide,
Forgetting leeches' penetration
So great our mutual concentration.

I didn't like it – not a bit,
And so prepared my plans to quit.
Thus there started midst the tents
My race against the elements.

Summon your imagination
'Ere you start your condemnation.
Visualise that swamped terrain
Pitch darkness, mud and blinding rain.

The shouts and cries of troops – five score,
All added to the river's roar.
Rushing forth in their profusion
Turning routine to confusion.

Till sergeant-major's frenzied roar,
Brings discipline to heel once more,
Turns the wild, excited mob
To soldiers eager for their job.

Through that numbing, driving rain,
Each took his load, then back again,
Stumbling, waist-deep through the tide
Officer – ranker – side by side.

Through the God-forsaken night,
Where none thought about his plight,
But swearing, as he groped his way
To cheat the river of its prey.

We won through at nigh on dawn,
And stood bedraggled, tired, forlorn,
Yes, we won – though someone said,
' 'Twas only by a shortened head.'

For then the river – banks a'breaking
Tore into the camp-site taking
All before it – trying to flatten
Tents – five and twenty – Indian pattern.

A small point here – it doesn't matter
I never thought that teeth could chatter,
Yet it's in this island's powers
When one stays wet for twenty hours.

Then Usk Valley superintendent,
Ignoring requisition – indent,
Processes unsatisfactory,
Housed us in his rubber factory.

197

I thus had time to cogitate,
On all my actions up to date,
And criticise impartially
My orders given so hurriedly,

Dub me smug, complacent swank,
Not fit to hold a captain's rank,
But my judgement, sans pretence,
Absolved me of all negligence.

But those so high and mightily
In CBO thought differently.
And hot-foot sent to question me
Staff-captain – one ex-QMG.

This worthy called me to the phone,
And adopting hectoring tone,
Advised that he would be with me
In two short shakes – right speedily.

Sadly then I shook my head.
'There are four floods to cross,' I said.
'That wont stop me!' swift came reply.
'I'm not the craven CLI!'

Yet – while waiting by the hour
For sound of his approaching car,
He telephoned once more to say
Some horrid floods had barred his way.

He made the grade some time next morn
Looking wet and tired and drawn.
'Why did you move?' he asked straightway.
I said, 'the flood washed us away.'

198

He nearly muttered, 'Dog – you lie!'
I could see it in his eye.
But instead he asked to see
The camp vacated recently.

On the way he tried to prove
There was no need for us to move.
He said had we dug deeper drains
We could have stemmed the monsoon rains.

I said, 'No tent drain would have caught a
Flood of ten feet six of water.'
(Temper making speech less warier)
I added, 'Quote me to Base Area.'

Vision won where speech had failed,
At flood he looked, at flood he quailed.
And looking, putting doubts to rout,
Turned his viewpoint arseabout.

Whereupon my doubts grew easy,
His manner changed to bright and breezy,
And boating round in frail canoe,
Gaily Kodaked all in view.

Remarking then, 'From what I've seen
You could have done with submarine,'
And with this joke – not very witty,
He beat it for Colombo City.

Late that night he rang again,
'I wished to speak to Captain Bayne,'
'Your wish is granted – speak my Lord,
I hang upon your every word.'

Cross patter then and bonhomie
Prevailed throughout his homily.
While he declared that come what might,
He'd have us home tomorrow night.

I demurred, when he had done,
'I am no Carter Patterson,
'And though the weather is improving
Ten tons of baggage takes some moving.

'It's not as if I've got dry roads,
And lorries for my several loads.
There are the floods – without canoe,
That yesterday put paid to you.'

Would he listen? Not a bit,
'You heard me pal – get on with it.'
Thus deciding to ignore,
His *Water*loo the day before.

I thereupon without much fuss
Began to plan my exodus.
And figured – being in the gravy
Would indent for the Allied Navy.

But changed my mind because these chaps,
Were dealing with the loathsome Japs.
So sought and found in lieu of slumber,
Canoes – outrigger – three in number.

Thus began my second shift,
'Neath clouds of grey that wouldn't lift,
In blinding rain that wouldn't stop,
Through rising flood that wouldn't drop.

Every ounce of every pound
Of arms, equipment, every round,
Kit and baggage, stores from Q,
Were *sailed* from camp to rendezvous.

No pleasure cruise in bright sunshine
No Hampton Court, no Serpentine,
Should be confused with that day's boating,
Unwieldy loads and craft just floating.

From dawn to dusk without a stop,
No lunch recess to chew a chop.
Through the day without a let-up,
That, then, was the grisly set-up.

My rescuer was due at four,
With lorries, Chevrolet, half score.
But he did not hove in view,
Till he was one hour overdue.

His smile was cordial, 'spite the wet
While asking if I'd finished yet.
But he doused his grin in one,
When I replied. 'I am *half* done.'

I said, 'Upon the farther shore,
Remains a slice of my Q store,
Which I will ferry here intac'
As darkness falls with sickening crack.'

Thereupon I sprang to boat,
Which waterlogged would barely float.
And bade my Charon brave the tide,
And take me to the other side.

201

Leaping off at destination,
Quickly formed rough estimation,
Calculating (roughly too)
We had about six trips to do.

Then overloading past the limit
Shouting, 'Boys, we'll sink or swim it,'
And by cramping stores up more
Cut our journey down to four.

So like sinking liner's skipper,
Was last to leave and seizing dipper
Frenzied baling put in hand,
Nor stopping till we sighted land.

But just before we made our landfall,
There smote upon my ear a catcall,
Followed up by screams of rage
I dare not quote or sully page.

The howls for full two minutes lasted
Came to ear, 'Where's Bayne, the (Censored)'
Either there had been calamity,
Or in our midst there stalked insanity.

Can you picture in your mind,
A Jekyll-Hyde, all Frankenstein'd,
Rasputin, Crippen, Satan's son
Beelzebub – rolled into one?

For such a fiend confronted me,
Not a sight for child, to see,
Bloodshot eyes – A' wildly rolling,
Temper long past all controlling.

'What the something, something blazes?'
Was the opening of his phrases,
Built up by most foul invective,
Panic banishing perspective.

I penetrated his disguise
Of frothing lips and rolling eyes,
Recognising him to be,
My worthy friend – the cap, G3.

So in front of my good men
He strafed me once and then again.
Inviting heaven to witness that
For this he'd have me on the mat.

All because I'd kept him waiting,
While I, flood negotiating,
Failed to keep our rendezvous,
Arranged by him – 'spite Waterloo.

But Reader – you have heard enough,
You must be bored with all this stuff.
So before you go quite gaga,
I'll terminate this lengthy saga.

Our journey home was calm enough,
And we were dumped with all our stuff.
Back again from where we'd started,
Angry? yes, but not downhearted.

The next day then on checking kit,
I found a minor deficit.
A hockey ball – a cleaning rod,
Reported lost, by act of God.

As result, I had to face
A board convened to try my case.
To find out why I shouldn't pay
For two small items washed away.

Base Area picked the Camp, not I,
They assured me it was dry,
Ignoring PD's warning clear,
That flood came thrice in every year.

They'd overlooked that in the strife,
I had not lost a single life,
They disbelieved that flood could rise,
In that short time to that great size.

In fact they'd overlooked things huge,
In eagerness to find a stooge
To take the rap and save their face,
Lest it result in fall from grace.

But that good enquiry board,
Heard me out without a word,
And finding I was not to blame,
They cleared the stigma from my name.

To Base Area I was sent,
Where brigadier – a real gent,
Read the file in triplicate,
Smiled and gave me chocolate.

G3 was not in happy mood,
He got a raspberry for being rude,
As result I'll skip our quarrel,
And finish up with this 'ere moral.

MORAL

There's a saying old and trite,
'The customer is always right.'
Forget it pal – you're CDF.*
Fob off madness – calm yourself,
Remember always -- day or night,
The *CDF* is always right.

(And how!)

ACLB
Jaela, 1942

---

*Ceylon Defence Force